Government Spending

Other Books of Related Interest

Opposing Viewpoints Series

Inflation

At Issue Series

Are Government Bailouts Effective?

Current Controversies Series

US Government Corruption

“Congress shall make no law … abridging the freedom of speech, or of the press.”

First Amendment to the US Constitution

The basic foundation of our democracy is the First Amendment guarantee of freedom of expression. The Opposing Viewpoints Series is dedicated to the concept of this basic freedom and the idea that it is more important to practice it than to enshrine it.

Government Spending

Noël Merino, Book Editor

GREENHAVEN PRESS
A part of Gale, Cengage Learning

Detroit • New York • San Francisco • New Haven, Conn • Waterville, Maine • London

Elizabeth Des Chenes, *Director, Publishing Solutions*

For more information, contact:
Greenhaven Press
27500 Drake Rd.
Farmington Hills, MI 48331-3535
Or you can visit our Internet site at gale.cengage.com.

Articles in Greenhaven Press anthologies are often edited for length to meet page requirements. In addition, original titles of these works are changed to clearly present the main thesis and to explicitly indicate the author's opinion. Every effort is made to ensure that Greenhaven Press accurately reflects the original intent of the authors. Every effort has been made to trace the owners of copyrighted material.

LIBRARY OF CONGRESS CATALOGING-IN-PUBLICATION DATA

Government spending / Noël Merino, book editor.
p. cm. -- (Opposing viewpoints)
Includes bibliographical references and index.
ISBN 978-0-7377-6322-5 (hardcover) -- ISBN 978-0-7377-6323-2 (pbk.)
1. Government spending policy--United States. 2. United States--Appropriations and expenditures. 3. Budget deficits--United States. I. Merino, Noël.
HJ7537.G686 2012
336.3'90973--dc23

2012023741

Printed in the United States of America
1 2 3 4 5 6 7 16 15 14 13 12

Contents

Chapter 4: How Must Government Spending Change to Meet Future Challenges?

Why Consider Opposing Viewpoints?

> *"The only way in which a human being can make some approach to knowing the whole of a subject is by hearing what can be said about it by persons of every variety of opinion and studying all modes in which it can be looked at by every character of mind. No wise man ever acquired his wisdom in any mode but this."*
>
> *John Stuart Mill*

In our media-intensive culture it is not difficult to find differing opinions. Thousands of newspapers and magazines and dozens of radio and television talk shows resound with differing points of view. The difficulty lies in deciding which opinion to agree with and which "experts" seem the most credible. The more inundated we become with differing opinions and claims, the more essential it is to hone critical reading and thinking skills to evaluate these ideas. Opposing Viewpoints books address this problem directly by presenting stimulating debates that can be used to enhance and teach these skills. The varied opinions contained in each book examine many different aspects of a single issue. While examining these conveniently edited opposing views, readers can develop critical thinking skills such as the ability to compare and contrast authors' credibility, facts, argumentation styles, use of persuasive techniques, and other stylistic tools. In short, the Opposing Viewpoints Series is an ideal way to attain the higher-level thinking and reading skills so essential in a culture of diverse and contradictory opinions.

In addition to providing a tool for critical thinking, Opposing Viewpoints books challenge readers to question their own strongly held opinions and assumptions. Most people form their opinions on the basis of upbringing, peer pressure, and personal, cultural, or professional bias. By reading carefully balanced opposing views, readers must directly confront new ideas as well as the opinions of those with whom they disagree. This is not to argue simplistically that everyone who reads opposing views will—or should—change his or her opinion. Instead, the series enhances readers' understanding of their own views by encouraging confrontation with opposing ideas. Careful examination of others' views can lead to the readers' understanding of the logical inconsistencies in their own opinions, perspective on why they hold an opinion, and the consideration of the possibility that their opinion requires further evaluation.

Evaluating Other Opinions

To ensure that this type of examination occurs, Opposing Viewpoints books present all types of opinions. Prominent spokespeople on different sides of each issue as well as well-known professionals from many disciplines challenge the reader. An additional goal of the series is to provide a forum for other, less known, or even unpopular viewpoints. The opinion of an ordinary person who has had to make the decision to cut off life support from a terminally ill relative, for example, may be just as valuable and provide just as much insight as a medical ethicist's professional opinion. The editors have two additional purposes in including these less known views. One, the editors encourage readers to respect others' opinions—even when not enhanced by professional credibility. It is only by reading or listening to and objectively evaluating others' ideas that one can determine whether they are worthy of consideration. Two, the inclusion of such viewpoints encourages the important critical thinking skill of objectively evaluating an author's credentials and bias. This evaluation will illuminate an author's reasons for taking a particular stance on an issue and will aid in readers' evaluation of the author's ideas.

It is our hope that these books will give readers a deeper understanding of the issues debated and an appreciation of the complexity of even seemingly simple issues when good and honest people disagree. This awareness is particularly important in a democratic society such as ours in which people enter into public debate to determine the common good. Those with whom one disagrees should not be regarded as enemies but rather as people whose views deserve careful examination and may shed light on one's own.

Thomas Jefferson once said that "difference of opinion leads to inquiry, and inquiry to truth." Jefferson, a broadly educated man, argued that "if a nation expects to be ignorant and free . . . it expects what never was and never will be." As individuals and as a nation, it is imperative that we consider the opinions of others and examine them with skill and discernment. The Opposing Viewpoints Series is intended to help readers achieve this goal.

David L. Bender and Bruno Leone,
Founders

Introduction

> *"Federal spending information is designed to inform the public on how and where tax dollars are being spent to provide transparency to the Federal government's operations."*
>
> *Jeffrey D. Zients, deputy director for management, US Office of Management and Budget*

Two key duties of government are to collect taxes from the populace and then direct how the money is spent by managing expenditures. In the United States, the federal government manages the spending on national programs, whereas state governments manage spending on local and state programs. In order to assess the federal government's current spending practices, it is necessary to see where the government currently spends its revenue. Looking at the major expenses, as well as the major sources of revenues, one can get a sense whether current spending practices need to be cut, increased, or reformed.

In fiscal year 2011, approximately 21 percent of the federal budget was spent on three health insurance programs: Medicare, Medicaid, and the Children's Health Insurance Program (CHIP). Medicare provides health insurance coverage to Americans over the age of sixty-five and those with disabilities. Medicaid provides funding for health-related services to low-income Americans through a program that the states manage, jointly funded by the federal and state governments. Similar to Medicaid and managed by the states, CHIP is a program that specifically provides health insurance to children who do not qualify for Medicaid but are financially needy. Thus, just over one-fifth of the federal budget goes toward health care costs of the needy and senior citizens.

In 2011, approximately 20 percent of the budget was used to pay Social Security benefits. Social Security provides benefits to retired workers and their dependents, deceased workers and their dependents, and disabled workers and their dependents. All Americans who have paid into the system through their employment taxes are eligible to receive benefits from the system at retirement, whether they have the economic need or not. Currently, the earliest age at which retirees are eligible for benefits—at a reduced rate—is sixty-two. Full retirement benefits depend on the retiree's year of birth, ranging from age sixty-five to sixty-seven.

Another 20 percent of the federal budget in 2011 was spent on defense and international security assistance. This spending pays for the costs of the Department of Defense, which funds the US Army, the Defense Intelligence Agency, and the National Security Agency, among others. This spending also includes military operations which, in 2011, funded the wars in Iraq and Afghanistan.

In 2011, the federal government spent 13 percent on safety net programs that provide economic support to Americans in need. These programs include tax credits, welfare, unemployment insurance, food stamps, low-income housing assistance, and other programs that aim to keep people out of poverty.

The remaining 26 percent of the budget was used for a variety of other programs. Seven percent of the federal budget in 2011 was used to pay benefits for federal retirees and veterans. Functioning much like Social Security, but for federal workers, these programs pay benefits to retired and disabled federal workers and veterans, as well as their eligible dependents. Six percent of the budget went toward the interest the United States owes on its debt. Three percent went to transportation infrastructure, and 2 percent each went to education and scientific research. The remaining spending used no more than 1 percent in each category.

The revenue collected by the US government goes to the aforementioned spending. Of the revenue collected by the US government in fiscal year 2010, the largest source—42 percent—was from individual income tax. The second largest was from payroll taxes—Medicare and Social Security taxes—at 40 percent. Nine percent came from corporate income tax and the remaining 9 percent came from other taxes. Although tax revenue is where all the cash to pay for programs comes from, it is not all the money that is spent. Since 1970 the US federal government has run deficit spending for all but four years, adding each year to the national debt.

Taxes fund a great amount of government spending, which gives US taxpayers an incentive to scrutinize expenditures and consider whether or not they are necessary. Furthermore, the fact that each year's spending tends to increase the debt makes taxpayers even more nervous—few want to pay more taxes to eliminate deficit spending but there is no consensus regarding where cuts should be made. *Opposing Viewpoints: Government Spending* scrutinizes government spending practices and offers criticism, praise, and suggestions for reform. Authors offer varying opinions on government spending in the following chapters: Is Current Government Spending Wasteful?, Should Government Spending Allow Deficits and Debt?, How Do Government Spending Policies Affect the Economy?, and How Must Government Spending Change to Meet Future Challenges?

Chapter 1

Is Current Government Spending Wasteful?

Chapter Preface

As a result of the US recession, state governments in recent years have become increasingly cash-strapped. State legislatures and governors have cut spending in a variety of areas because of a dearth of revenue. One of the programs that has come under attack in a few states is unemployment compensation.

Unemployment insurance is a program jointly financed by the federal and state governments. Employers fund the program through payroll taxes and when workers become unemployed through no fault of their own, they can file for unemployment insurance and receive a portion of their previous pay for a certain number of weeks. Recipients of this temporary financial assistance are expected to look for work, and when a new paid job commences the unemployment compensation ends.

States administer the unemployment insurance program, and eligibility, benefit amount, and length of benefit are all determined by state law. The weekly benefit amount varies widely among the states. Arizona, for instance, pays a maximum benefit of $240 per week, whereas New Jersey's maximum benefit is $611 per week. Historically, most states paid unemployment benefits for a maximum of twenty-six weeks, with extended benefits programs available during periods of high unemployment. In recent years, however, numerous states have lowered the period of maximum benefits. In 2011, Florida cut its twenty-six-week maximum length of benefit to a range of twelve to twenty-three weeks, depending on past earnings. In Michigan, the maximum length of benefits ranges from fourteen to twenty weeks and in Washington from one to twenty-six weeks.

Some people believe cutting unemployment benefits is a good way to save money and get people back to work. During a 2010 Senate debate, Senator Jon Kyl, a Republican from Arizona, claimed, "Continuing to pay people unemployment compensation is a disincentive for them to seek new work." Senator Max

Baucus, a Democrat from Montana, disagreed: "Nothing could be further from the truth. I don't know anybody who's out of work and is receiving some unemployment insurance believes that that payment is sufficient not to find a job. The payments are so much lower than any salary or wage would be, it's just ridiculous." The wisdom of cutting unemployment insurance depends on the actual impact of the benefits on the recipient.

Debates about government-spending programs often focus on a similar issue: Does the spending achieve a social goal without causing an additional cost? In the case of unemployment insurance, someone taking Kyl's point of view might argue that the overall impact of unemployment benefits is to keep people out of work, depress the economy, and waste taxpayer money. Someone with Baucus's point of view might claim that unemployment benefits keep people out of poverty (and, thus, off the welfare rolls), allow them a bridge to get back to work, and are a good investment of taxpayer money. The authors in this chapter offer differing views on the justification of current government spending programs.

Viewpoint 1

"Federal workers continue to earn a pay premium of around 12 percent over private workers."

Government Employees Are Overcompensated

Andrew G. Biggs and Jason Richwine

In the following viewpoint, Andrew G. Biggs and Jason Richwine argue against claims that public sector workers are underpaid. Biggs and Richwine contend that when level of skill is compared to the private sector, federal employees are overcompensated. State and local employees, the authors claim, are also overcompensated once you take into account all benefits received. Biggs is a resident scholar at the American Enterprise Institute, and Richwine is a senior policy analyst of empirical studies at the Heritage Foundation.

As you read, consider the following questions:

1. According to Biggs and Richwine, the typical federal employee in 2008 received a total annual compensation totaling over what amount?
2. What percent of federal employees is at least one level of responsibility above comparable private-sector workers, according to a study cited in the viewpoint?

Andrew G. Biggs and Jason Richwine, "Those Underpaid Government Workers." *American Spectator*, September 2010. http://spectator.org.

3. When the full value of all entitlements is included, the authors claim that total compensation for state and local government employees rises by what percent?

What recession? Government workers are probably wondering what all the fuss is about. The private sector has lost 2.5 million jobs since the Obama administration's stimulus bill was passed, while the public sector—federal, state, and local government combined—has added 416,000 jobs over the same period. Although 85 percent of Americans work for private employers, the administration's own Recovery Act database admits that four out of five jobs "created or saved" were in government. Likewise, average pay has risen in the federal, state, and local government, while private sector wages have fallen. More jobs, better security, and rising wages—it's boom time in the public sector.

The Controversy over Public Sector Workers

Ordinary Americans, along with a small group of elected officials from both parties, have finally been stirred to action. New Jersey's Republican governor Chris Christie is a leader in taking on public sector unions over performance, pay, and pensions, and California governor Arnold Schwarzenegger has cajoled public employee unions into accepting pension reductions. Even some Democratic appointees—such as Washington, D.C., public schools chancellor Michelle Rhee, who recently took the unprecedented step of firing 241 underperforming teachers—seem to have had enough.

Despite this, defenders of public sector workers continue to argue that they are *underpaid*. Union representative Colleen Kelley, in a recent letter to the *Wall Street Journal*, cited federal statistics claiming that federal workers are paid 22 percent less than private sector employees doing similar jobs. Likewise, recent studies from liberal think tanks claim state and local employees receive significantly lower pay and benefits than private workers. Until these arguments are addressed, fully and directly, the group of policy makers with the mettle to tackle public sector pay will remain small.

A raw comparison between the wages of federal and private workers suggests there is no contest at all. The typical federal employee received a salary of more than $79,000 in 2008, with benefits raising total annual compensation to more than $119,000. The typical private sector worker, by contrast, received pay of around $50,000 and total compensation of just under $60,000. Moreover, *USA Today* recently reported that federal employees receive higher average salaries than private sector workers in 180 of 216 comparable occupations. These numbers seem to speak for themselves.

The Issue of Skill

Defenders of federal pay are quick to point out, however, that federal employees are more skilled than the typical worker in the private sector—in other words, they deserve more money. As OMB [Office of Management and Budget] director Peter Orszag argued, "A comparison of federal and private sector pay . . . is misleading because the employees hired by the federal government often have higher levels of education than their counterparts in the private sector."

Orszag is right: we do need to account for skill differences in the federal workforce, which is older, more educated, and more white-collar than workers in the private sector. But the question then becomes whether these differences are enough to account for the huge disparity in pay. Using the Census Bureau's Current Population Survey, which includes earnings and demographic data on tens of thousands of workers spread across the public and private sectors, we can control for differences in education, work experience, race, gender, marital status, immigration status, region of residence, and several other variables. After doing so, we can see whether the pay gap between federal and private sector workers remains.

This "human capital" approach to explaining wage variation, the overwhelming preference of labor economists, assumes that in competitive labor markets individuals with the same productivity will command similar salaries, even if they work different jobs. The human capital method is commonly used by economists in other contexts—such as determining whether union members receive higher pay than similarly qualified non-union members, or whether women and minorities receive lower pay than comparable white males.

A Remaining Disparity

Even after including the full range of control variables in our own analysis, we found that federal workers continue to earn a pay premium of around 12 percent over private workers. In other words, someone in the private sector has to work an average of 13.5 months to earn what an equally skilled federal worker makes in 12 months. This is not a novel result by any means. Academic economists have been studying federal/private pay disparities since the 1970s, and they generally find a premium in the range of 10 to 20 percent.

Though the data are less precise, benefits like retirement contributions and health insurance rates are also more generous for federal employees. We have calculated that the annual overpayment of salary and benefits to federal workers comes to more than $14,000 per worker, totaling nearly $40 billion per year.

This does not mean everyone in the federal government should get an automatic pay cut. In fact, our data suggest the brightest people—research scientists, for example—receive no premium and may even suffer a penalty when they work for the government. If the federal government rewarded skills the way the private sector does, wages would adjust in different ways for different workers. Overall, however, total compensation would go down by around 12 percent, taxpayers would save tens of billions of dollars each year, and the federal government would regain some much-needed fiscal credibility.

The Charge That Federal Workers Are Underpaid

But where do claims that federal workers are underpaid come from? From the President's Pay Agent—not an actual person, but an obscure function headed by the Secretary of Labor and the directors of the Office of Management and Budget and the Office of Personnel Management. Relying heavily on the recommendations of the Federal Salary Council, a panel of labor union representatives, the Pay Agent submits an annual report to the president suggesting how much to increase federal pay. The 2009 report claims, remarkably, that federal workers are *underpaid* by more than 22 percent relative to the private sector.

Before we discuss the reasons for the large discrepancy between the Pay Agent's results and ours, consider how implausible the 22 percent figure actually is. Why would millions of federal employees accept such a low wage if they could earn thousands more in the private sector? A desire to serve the public can go only so far. High-ranking government officials are no doubt attracted to the power and prestige of their jobs, but what about the vast number of unremarkable paper-pushing jobs the government offers? What is so attractive about these positions that justifies taking 78 cents on the dollar?

Barring an almost unbelievable level of civic-mindedness on the part of federal employees, either federal positions offer non-wage compensation that outweighs a 22 percent salary gap—in which case these workers aren't truly underpaid—or the 22 percent salary gap figure is wrong to begin with. We think both are true.

The Problem with the Pay Agent

The Pay Agent's figure is inaccurate because of the method it uses to compare pay in each sector. Rather than using skills like education and experience to identify productivity, as most economists recommend, the Pay Agent relies on a survey of job descriptions in various localities. For example, suppose the federal government employs an accountant in Chicago. In order to determine how much to pay him, the government would look at the job descriptions of private sector accountants in the Chicago area. It would try to find the subset of accountants who seem to have the same responsibilities as the government hire, then take the average salary in that set.

Though it sounds reasonable enough, the process is highly subjective. Positions that seem "comparable" on paper could be much different in practice, and some federal jobs have no private sector counterparts. How much should an intelligence analyst be paid based on his job description? Most importantly, unlike the human capital approach, the Pay Agent cannot distinguish between high- and low-productivity workers in the same position. It is just assumed that a particular job description leads to a certain level of output.

That is a rather poor assumption, because government appears to systematically promote employees to higher positions than they could hold in the private sector. An individual who would serve as a junior accountant in the private sector, for example, might be a senior accountant for government. One study found that 77 percent of federal employees are at least one level of responsibility above that of comparable workers in the private sector. This means government positions may appear underpaid relative to comparable private sector occupations, but the individuals filling those positions could be overpaid relative to what they would earn outside of government. The Pay Agent's method is inherently oblivious to this problem.

Even the federal Pay Agent's own analysts have expressed strong reservations about the government's system for setting wages. The 2008 report states, "We continue to have major methodological concerns about the underlying model for estimating pay gaps." Each report between 2001 and 2008 included some version of this warning. Curiously, the first report produced by the Obama administration omitted any mention of reform.

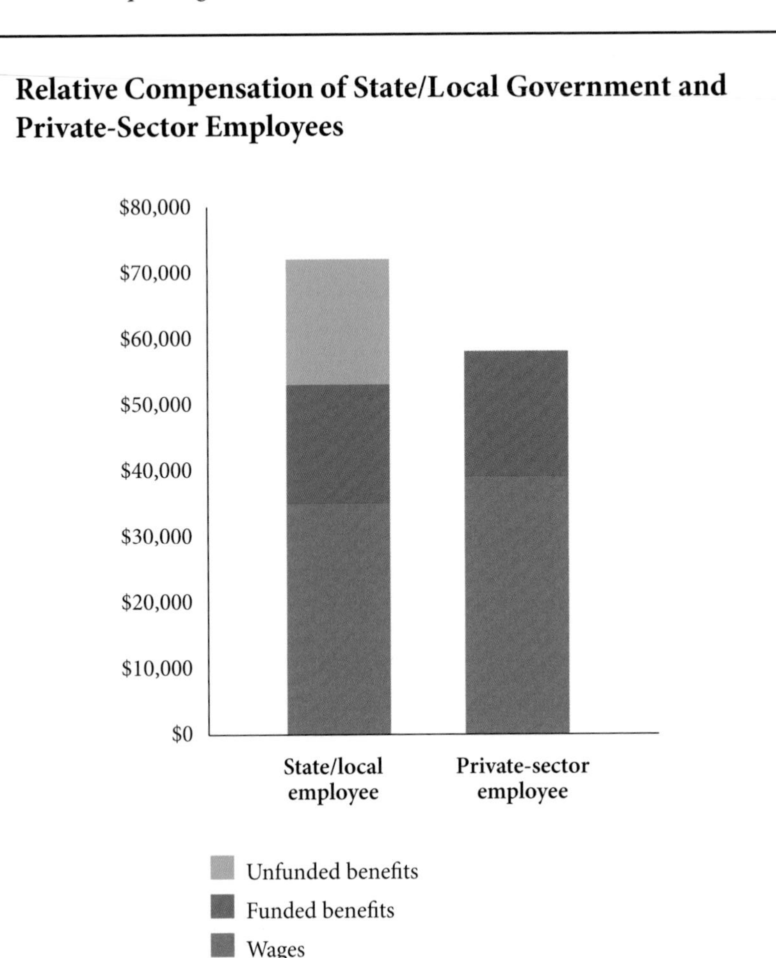

TAKEN FROM: Andrew G. Biggs, "Are Government Workers Underpaid? No," *American*, www.american.com.

The Popularity of Government Jobs

The pay agent's figures are even less believable when we consider just how popular government jobs are. At the beginning of this year [2010], federal workers were only one-third as likely as private sector workers to quit their jobs, a difference that exists during good economic times as well as bad. Since perhaps the most common reason for quitting a job is to take another that offers some combination of better wages, benefits, and working conditions, the fact that federal workers don't jump ship implies there is usually no better deal out there. Government job postings also receive considerably more applications than private sector openings, again pointing to their attractiveness.

In 1988, economist Alan Krueger—currently serving the Obama administration as chief economist at the U.S. Treasury Department—examined the wages of two different groups of people who were laid off from their private sector jobs. One group took new jobs in the private sector, while the other group became federal employees. The latter group, unsurprisingly, made significantly more money after the job change than the former. These results, together with the evidence on quit rates, application quantity, and sheer gut-level plausibility, form a solid block of evidence supporting the findings of superior federal pay, benefits, and working conditions.

Comparisons for state and local government workers are more complicated, because here it is mainly benefits, not wages, that make government work attractive. John Schmitt of the left-leaning Center for Economic and Policy Research (CEPR) recently wrote, "When state and local government employees are compared to private sector workers with similar characteristics, state and local workers actually earn less, on average, than their private sector counterparts." In contrast to the federal case, there are hard numbers to back up this claim—at least when the case is limited to wages.

State and Local Government Jobs

While the human capital approach shows a 12 percent wage premium for federal government employees, it tends to show a pay *penalty* at the state and local level of 10 to 12 percent. It is not clear why state and local workers receive lower wages than federal employees—competition among the states might play a role in keeping salaries in line—but unions and liberal think tanks have seized on this finding to claim that state and local workers are undercompensated.

This conclusion does not survive scrutiny. For one thing, state and local employees are five times more likely to be covered by union contracts than private sector employees. Since union members predictably receive higher pay than non-union members, policies to allow collective bargaining by government employees are tantamount to decisions to raise pay. While some analysts would have you believe that state and local employees are paid just like private sector workers, the truth is that they are paid more like *unionized* private sector workers, which is a different kettle of fish.

Moreover, at both the state and local level, generous benefits are likely to more than make up for any salary gap, large or small. While studies by think tanks like the CEPR claim that benefit levels are comparable between state/local and private sector workers, they employ a serious methodological error.

The Comparison of Benefits

The basic method of comparing benefits for public and private sector workers is simple: use data on what employers pay for each employee's fringe benefits, such as health insurance and pensions. In the private sector this method usually works fine. Employee benefits take the form of an up-front payment—a matching contribution to a 401(k) account, for example—not an IOU like a pension plan.

In the public sector, however, this approach can be quite misleading because a good portion of government employees' benefits come in the form of defined benefit pensions and retiree health coverage. These benefits are both highly generous and severely underfunded, which means that what government employers currently pay for these benefits significantly understates the benefits employees will become entitled to and must eventually collect.

Public sector pension plans reported unfunded liabilities of approximately $500 billion as of 2008. When measured by the more rigorous standards required for private pension plans, however, public pensions are underfunded by more than $3 trillion. Added to this is approximately $500 billion in unfunded obligations for generous retiree health benefits, which provide full coverage from the age of retirement through Medicare eligibility at 65, then supplemental coverage thereafter.

Unlike programs like Social Security, where underfunding can mean benefit cuts, accrued public sector pension benefits are in most states guaranteed either by law or by state constitutions. In other words, state government employees are eligible for $3.5 trillion more in benefits than labor compensation data would suggest, because these reflect only what employers do pay, not what they *should* pay if they are to meet their obligations. When the full value of pension and retiree health entitlements is included, total compensation for state and local employees rises by approximately 25 percent, putting these employees thousands of dollars ahead of their private sector counterparts.

Even leaving wages and benefits aside, the intangible perks of public employment—automatic annual raises, flexible hours, generous paid vacation time—provide significant added value. Then there is the near-certainty of not being fired. The annual rate of layoffs and firings in 2009 was 24 percent in the private sector but only 7 percent in state and federal government. Given that the average duration of unemployment in 2009 was more than 22 weeks—and is even higher today—this additional job security for public sector employees has an expected value of more than $8,000 for a typical federal employee. In practice, individuals would gladly pay even more for this insurance, since layoffs and firings tend to happen at the worst possible times—when the economy is down and millions of other workers are looking for jobs.

The Effects of Public Sector Overcompensation

The cost of public sector overcompensation goes beyond higher taxes. Economists Yann Algan, Pierre Cahuc, and Andre

Zylberberg write in the *Economic Policy Journal* that, on average, "creation of 100 public jobs may have eliminated about 150 private sector jobs, slightly decreased labor market participation, and increased by about 33 the number of unemployed workers." Their conclusion, drawn from data on 17 Organisation for Economic Co-operation and Development (OECD) countries over the period 1960 to 2000, is that attractive pay and conditions in public employment make private sector positions less attractive to job seekers. Given what we have seen regarding compensation at all levels of government, that is easy to believe.

Moreover, a number of studies, including by the OECD and the International Monetary Fund, have shown that countries that balance their budgets through reductions in social transfer programs and the government wage bill—that is, the number of government workers and the generosity of their pay—are more successful in reducing government debt than those that raise taxes. The reason may be that, because government pay is among the toughest of expenditures to reduce, governments that succeed in cutting it establish credibility with the public and build confidence with financial markets.

For perhaps the first time, a widespread swath of ordinary Americans appear ready to seriously reconsider the pay, benefits, and job security granted to public employees. With private sector workers and their families bearing the brunt of the recession, the existence of a seemingly protected class of government employees has generated a response that goes well beyond the inefficient use of taxpayer dollars to a sense of fundamental unfairness. But like government largesse in other forms, excessive public pay has some tenacious supporters. Public sector unions, for one, appreciate the extra cash, and even non-union government employees tend to have disproportionate political power. The question of public sector pay will be decided by how Americans vote and, perhaps more importantly, by the courage of public officials after the votes are counted.

"We should in many cases be hiring many more bureaucrats—and paying more to get better ones—not cutting their numbers and freezing their pay."

Government Spending Is Not Wasted on the Federal Workforce

John Gravois

In the following viewpoint, John Gravois argues that shrinking the federal workforce in an attempt to save money will actually have the opposite effect. Gravois contends that cuts to the federal workforce since the 1990s have resulted in higher costs, risks to the military, a lack of adequate inspectors for oil wells, and a lack of regulation in the financial markets. Gravois claims that the detrimental effects of workforce cuts are not worth the small amount of money saved. He concludes that the federal workforce actually needs to be expanded. Gravois is an editor of the Washington Monthly.

As you read, consider the following questions:

1. According to Gravois, what cuts in the federal workforce were called for in the proposed CUTS Act?

John Gravois, "More Bureaucrats, Please," *Washington Monthly*, March–April 2011.

2. Cost overruns for weapons contracts increased by how much between 2000 and 2009, according to Gravois?
3. According to the author, what has happened to the size of the federal workforce since the 1960s?

In the preamble to its December [2010] report on how to wrangle America's fiscal crisis, President [Barack] Obama's deficit commission conjured the image of a family hunkered down around the kitchen table, "making tough choices about what they hold most dear and what they can learn to live without." The attempt to make fiscal reform sound human sized—like something out of a very special episode of *The Waltons*—was understandable, given the colossal abstractions that followed in the report's recommendations ("Extend Medicaid drug rebate to dual eligibles in Part D;" "Move to a competitive territorial tax system"). But at least one of the bipartisan commission's ideas did possess a kind of after-supper, intuitive appeal: cutting the federal workforce by 10 percent and freezing federal salaries.

The Calls for Downsizing

In tough times, everyone understands downsizing. If the symbolism of belt tightening weren't so powerful, President Obama probably wouldn't have announced his call for a two-year freeze on federal salaries in November. The actual savings associated with the move are fairly trivial in the grand scheme, but the signal was bright and clear. "All of us are called on to make some sacrifices," Obama said to the cameras. "And I'm asking civil servants to do what they've always done—play their part."

The new Republican majority in the [US] House [of Representatives] has, naturally, been happy to take up this theme. In January [2011], Representative Kevin Brady of Texas introduced the too cleverly named Cut Unsustainable and Top-heavy Spending (CUTS) Act, whose provisions closely mirrored the debt commission's plan for downsizing the federal workforce: a 10 percent cut through attrition, and a three-year pay freeze.

Then the Republican Study Committee, a congressional group crowded with Tea Party freshmen, upped the ante, calling for a 15 percent slash to the civil service amid a long menu of other spending cuts that, while drastic, would actually do little to ease the workload of the federal bureaucracy. In both cases, the sales pitch for gutting the civil service was more or less the same. "There's not a business in America that's survived this recession without right-sizing its workforce," Brady told the *Washington Post* after introducing his bill. "The federal government can't be the exception."

The Reality of Cuts to the Federal Workforce

The problem is that, as employers go, the federal government is in fact pretty exceptional. A corporation can shed workers and then revise its overall business strategy accordingly. A strapped city government can lay off a few street sweepers and then elect to sweep the streets less often. But federal agencies are governed by statutory requirements. Unless Congress changes those statutes, federal agencies' mandates—their work assignments—stay the same, regardless of how many people are on hand to carry them out. Medicare checks still have to go out within thirty days of a claim, offshore oil wells still need to be inspected, soldiers in Afghanistan still need to be provisioned, Social Security databases still need to be maintained, and on and on. "It raises the hairs on my neck when I hear people say we've got to do more with less," says John Palguta, a vice president for policy at the Partnership for Public Service, a nonprofit focused on the government workforce. "The logical conclusion is we're going to do more with nothing."

In practice, cutting civil servants often means either adding private contractors or—in areas where the government plays a regulatory function—resorting to the belief that industries have a deep capacity to police themselves. (This idea, of course, has taken some dings in recent years.) And though contractors can be enormously useful, they too have to be, well, governed. "You can cut and cut and cut and try to streamline the government workforce, but at some point you lose the ability to oversee the money that you're spending, and that puts everything at greater risk," says Don Kettl, dean of the University of Maryland's School of Public Policy. "The opportunities for program failure and waste of public dollars grow exponentially."

In other words, if Congress and the White House agree to substantial cuts in the federal workforce but don't also agree to eliminate programs and reduce services, the end result could be *more* spending and deficits, not less. Strange as it may sound, to get a grip on costs, we should in many cases be hiring many more bureaucrats—and paying more to get better ones—not cutting their numbers and freezing their pay. Because in many parts of government, the bureaucracy has already crossed that dangerous threshold beyond which further cuts can only mean greater risk of a breakdown. Indeed, much of the runaway spending we've seen over the past decade is the result of our having crossed that line years ago—the last time there was a Democrat in the White House, a divided government, and calls for slashing the federal workforce in the air.

The National Partnership for Reinventing Government

One night in the autumn of 1993, Americans watching their bedroom TV sets caught an unusual appearance by Vice President Al Gore on *Late Night with David Letterman*. He had come to smash an ashtray. In an unlikely pop tutorial on the federal bureaucracy, Gore explained to the studio audience that any time a hapless federal acquisitions officer—someone in charge of buying stuff for the government—faced the thankless task of purchasing an ashtray, he had to pore through ten pages of bureaucratese to find out what specifications the thing had to meet. There were even mandatory instructions for ashtray safety testing. When smashed with a hammer, the official writ had it, "the specimen should break into a small number of irregularly shaped pieces, no greater than 35." With that, Gore and Letterman gamely strapped on safety goggles and conducted an in-studio ashtray safety test—all to lampoon the manner in which a fusty bureaucracy did its shopping.

Gore's stunt was meant to promote a new White House initiative called the National Partnership for Reinventing Government. With the Cold War fading from the rearview mirror and defense spending ratcheting down, the brand-new Clinton administration wanted to seize their moment to modernize the government through a system of information-age reforms. (One example: giving civil servants the freedom to go buy office supplies—or ashtrays—at their local Staples using a federal credit card.) Reinventing Government's noble, liberal aim was to restore public faith in federal institutions. But it also came to serve a more tactical purpose. As the Gingrich revolution swept Washington, Reinventing Government allowed the White House to politically outflank a GOP eager to gut the bureaucracy for the sake of gutting. A central argument for the initiative became, "If you fix the process, you don't need the people." When the initiative tallied its accomplishments in 1998, at the top of its list was cutting the federal workforce by 351,000 civil servants.

A Decrease in the Defense Acquisitions Workforce

One of the greatest targets of all those cuts was the Defense Department's acquisitions workforce—the lowly ashtray buyers, yes, but also the cadre of professionals who write the military's more sophisticated contracts for goods or services, negotiate their terms, manage their execution, and audit their end results. This tribe of bureaucrats came under fire on multiple fronts. The biggest blow came not from Reinventing Government, but from the Republican Congress, which in 1996 ordered a 25 percent decrease in the Defense acquisitions workforce before the year 2000. With that plus other workforce reductions that had already taken place earlier in the decade, the number of Defense contracting officers fell by 50 percent—from 460,000 to 230,000—over the course of the 1990s.

It turned out to be a case of modernization gone horribly awry. At roughly the same time as the Defense contract management workforce was being hollowed out, the military was reorganizing itself around a vastly increased dependence on outside contractors. The balance of "acquisitions" was shifting from the relatively straightforward purchase of goods (Gore's ashtray) to the more sophisticated enlistment of services (the rapid construction of a field power station). And the weapons systems that the Pentagon was buying were only becoming more technologically complex. If anything, the workforce needed beefed-up expertise. "A lot of people in acquisition and procurement were people with a high school education," says John Kamensky, a senior fellow at the IBM Center for the Business of Government who was among the leaders of Reinventing Government. "What we needed was people with degrees who knew how to manage contracts." But instead the workforce simply eroded.

The Negative Effects of a Trimmed Workforce

The signs of impending danger were already apparent in 2000. "Staffing reductions have clearly outpaced productivity increases," said a Pentagon inspector general's report that year, citing contract backlogs and rising costs. From there, things only got worse. First came the terror attacks of September 11, 2001, then the war in Afghanistan, and then the war in Iraq, all under the watch of a president—George W. Bush—whose administration favored the use of contractors wherever possible. Defense spending soared, but the diminished contracting workforce was largely passed over in all the hubbub. "After 9/11, the Defense Department chose to increase war-fighter abilities," says Jacques Gansler, a former undersecretary of defense for acquisition, technology, and logistics under [President Bill] Clinton. "And yet in

Iraq and Afghanistan we actually have more contractors on the battlefield than people in uniform."

In 2007, Gansler was appointed by the secretary of the army to lead a commission looking into the problem of contracting in Iraq and Afghanistan. The commission's report called the buildup to the crisis a "perfect storm": the workload of contracting officers had increased sevenfold in recent years, but their ranks had never recovered from cutbacks in the '90s. "Essentially," the report said, "the Army sent a skeleton contracting force into theater." The battlefield had become a complex, uncoordinated, and chaotic overlay of soldiers under command and private contractors roaming free. "When the critical need is to get a power station running, and there are no resources to monitor contractor performance," the report said, "only the contractor knows whether the completed work is being sabotaged nightly." For the military at war, the job of getting what it vitally needed from contractors had become a "pickup game."

But perhaps the most ringing effect of the hollow acquisitions workforce is higher costs. Every year, the Government Accountability Office [GAO] analyzes a portfolio of major weapons contracts to see how the Pentagon is handling its acquisitions process, and the past decade has seen a staggering trend of increased cost overruns. In 2000, the average weapons system contract ultimately cost 6 percent more than originally projected. In 2009, the average weapons program ended up costing 25 percent more. Cost overruns for that year alone amounted to $296 billion. Among the causes of the problem, the GAO's 2009 report cited "shortages of acquisition professionals" as well as "degradation in oversight, delays in certain management and contracting activities, increased workloads for existing staff, and a reliance on support contractors to fill some voids."

Similar Problems Elsewhere

The acquisitions nightmare is, unfortunately, not just a problem at the Pentagon. For years now, the FBI [Federal Bureau of

Investigation] has famously (and expensively) struggled to create a centralized, web-based case management system—in large part, according to the agency's inspector general, because of "weak government contract management." Or consider the case of the Coast Guard: after 9/11, when the agency was subsumed under the new Department of Homeland Security, its leaders secured $24 billion to refurbish the Guard's badly antiquated fleet. But having been subject to the same 1990s personnel cuts as the Pentagon, the Coast Guard didn't even *have* a dedicated acquisitions department. So the agency seized on an "innovative" solution: Northrop Grumman and Lockheed Martin managed the contracting themselves. The result was a disaster. The extended hulls on a fleet of refurbished boats buckled, while eight large new ships that had been commissioned came in with serious design flaws, causing huge delays and cost overruns in the hundreds of millions of dollars.

In the realm of acquisitions, then, elected officials whittled down the ranks of key personnel just as the government was becoming strategically married to the use of outsourcing—and just *before* a national crisis dumped a ten-year avalanche of work on anyone involved in managing contracts for the government. A decrease in the workforce coincided with an increase in responsibility—and a rise in stray costs. As it happens, an uncannily similar pattern has played out in the biggest regulatory failures of recent years.

A Lack of Inspectors

Chronic manpower problems at the Minerals Management Service—the office within the Interior Department charged with regulating offshore oil wells—stretched all the way back to the 1990s, when a long boom in deepwater drilling coincided with a bust in the agency's funding. In December of 1996, the year when the agency's budget bottomed out, the *Houston Chronicle* reported that offshore fires, explosions, and blowouts had increased by 81 percent in the years of heightening offshore oil extraction since 1992. Yet over the remainder of the decade, the frequency of surprise inspections took a nosedive and never recovered. "Precisely when the need for regulatory oversight intensified," wrote the National Oil Spill Commission in its report this January [2011], "the government's capacity for oversight diminished."

The situation barely improved in the 2000s. The *Washington Post* reentry reported that, between 1988 and 2008, the number of deep-sea oil extraction projects in the Gulf of Mexico increased tenfold. But the number of inspectors assigned to the region barely budged. By the time of last year's [2010] Deepwater Horizon oil spill—the largest environmental disaster in U.S. history—Minerals Management had fifty-five inspectors matched against some *3,000* far-flung offshore facilities across the Gulf—a ratio of 1 to 55.

What's worse, those inspectors were woefully undertrained—they complained of it themselves—and significantly underpaid. As oil companies moved into deeper and deeper water, their drilling technology—including the now-infamous "blowout preventers"—far outpaced the inspectors' knowledge and the agency's technical regulations. Some inspectors "noted that they rely on industry representatives to explain the technology at a facility," the commission report says. And at a time when even the industry struggled to recruit enough qualified engineers to staff its expansion, the regulator stood virtually no chance in the competition for talent. Minerals Management "has difficulty recruiting inspectors," said the Department of Interior's inspector general in congressional testimony last year. "Industry tends to offer considerably higher wages and bonuses."

Is it any mystery, then, why the Minerals Management Service failed to prevent a blowout in the Macondo Well 5,000 feet undersea? Quite apart from other huge problems facing the small agency (the conflicts of interest inherent in its lucrative royalty-collecting program, its place in a Department of Interior largely run by energy lobbyists during the Bush administration, and the much-reported "culture of substance abuse and promiscuity" in certain suboffices), its manpower issues alone would seem fatal enough.

The Securities and Exchange Commission

Much the same pattern held in the Securities and Exchange Commission's [SEC's] oversight of the financial sector in the run-up to the financial crisis. In the early Bush years, SEC Chairman William H. Donaldson understood that his famously understaffed and outmatched agency was having to oversee increasing volumes of ever-more-complex financial activity. "There was a real need to increase the staff," says Donaldson. "We had to really fight to get that done." In addition to adding personnel, Donaldson created a central Office of Risk Assessment to monitor warning signals across the SEC's various divisions. And he set about trying to hire a few brokerage and investment pros familiar with the kinds of "innovative" financial instruments then sweeping Wall Street (an uphill battle in an agency predisposed to hiring lawyers).

While Donaldson was playing catch-up by beefing up his staff, the SEC was also fatefully handed a key new responsibility. The European Union had just told America's largest financial holding companies—the likes of Bear Stearns, Goldman Sachs, and Lehman Brothers—that, if they wanted to keep doing business on the Continent, they would need to submit to "consolidated supervision" from an American regulatory agency. (Their subsidiaries were regulated by various agencies, but the holding companies as such were not.) And so in 2004 the five biggest investment firms crafted a voluntary arrangement with the SEC that afforded the regulatory agency unprecedented access to their books. But there was also a riskier side to the bargain: the deal significantly eased the limits on how much debt the major firms could take on, freeing up billions of dollars—usually held in reserve as an asset cushion—to be invested in the kinds of exotic financial instruments that would become household names after the crash in 2008.

The SEC might have been able to handle this perilous and demanding set of new responsibilities had it continued down the road Donaldson laid out. But instead, between 2005 and 2007, the agency lost about 10 percent of its total personnel due to a hiring freeze, including 11 percent of its enforcement division. According to the Financial Crisis Inquiry Commission [FCIC], the new supervisory program over the big-five investment firms, which relied heavily on the firms' own computer models and self-reporting, was "troubled from the start." In the summer of 2005, Donaldson resigned and was replaced by the former Republican Congressman Christopher Cox, for whom the supervisory program was "not a priority," according to the *New York Times*. "Preoccupied with its own staff reorganization," the FCIC says, the supervisory program went more than a year without conducting a major examination.

The Cost of the Financial Crisis

All of this coincided, under Cox's leadership, with an agency outlook more generally in line with the Bush-era faith in laissez-faire oversight and industry self-policing. In a move that many have highlighted, Cox all but dismantled the Office of Risk Assessment that Donaldson had set up, reducing its staff to four part-time workers, according to *Portfolio* magazine. "The exact places where you didn't want to make cuts were in the risk assessment and financial products area," says James D. Cox, an expert on securities law at Duke University (and no relation to the former chairman). In 2005 alone, enforcement cases fell by 9 percent.

By the time that Bear Stearns collapsed in 2008, by many reports the commission's staff was already badly demoralized. In an op-ed headlined "Muzzling the Watchdog," three former heads of the commission wrote that the SEC "lacks the money, manpower, and tools it needs to do its job." (Pathetically outmoded technology was another major problem.) "You never have enough people, but if you could bump up enforcement levels, say, 20%, it would make a huge difference," a former senior counsel to the enforcement division named Bruce Carton told *Time* magazine. "Tweaking policies won't replace more manpower and training."

If there were any place where the federal government might have had a fighting chance to fend off or at least ameliorate the worst financial crisis since the Great Depression, it was at the SEC in the mid-2000s. Instead, the SEC divested itself of personnel and initiative. Consider the breathtaking consequences: not just the $700 billion bailout (most of which has been or will be paid back), but $400 billion in lost federal revenue as a result of the recession (that's in 2009 alone) and the $800 billion stimulus to get us out of it. Suddenly, shaving a few million dollars from the overhead costs of the SEC doesn't sound like much of a bargain.

The Demands for Austerity

The average voter may imagine federal bureaucracies as overstaffed, full of people leaning on their rakes and sharpening their pencils. But the truth is, most agencies are, if anything, understaffed. The government has grown tremendously in its spending and scope since the 1960s, and the population of the nation has grown by a margin of 100 million people, but the size of the federal workforce has remained remarkably static at about 2 million. Since coming into office two years ago, the Obama administration has bumped up staff levels by about 100,000, in part through "in-sourcing"—bringing back into the civil service inherently governmental work that had been farmed out to contractors. If this leads to better management, it could well mean a stanching of some of the cost overruns and regulatory failures that have been causing the government to bleed red ink. Today's mindless demands for austerity, however, could reverse this trend.

This is not to say that there aren't big bureaucratic reforms that need to be made that could lead to people losing their jobs.

Many agencies, for instance, exhibit excessive layering in their management ranks (think job titles that start with "deputy-" or "under-"). And if Congress and the administration could agree to lift some of the outdated procedural requirements and redundant reporting demands that are the bane of the average civil servant's life, it might be possible for agencies to fulfill their mission as well or better with fewer people.

But reforms like this almost never happen. Instead, what you usually get are demands like what we're now seeing in Congress for across-the-board cuts in the workforce. This is often accomplished through attrition and incentives for early retirement. But the people most likely to walk away in those cases are the ones most confident of their ability to land a job in the private sector—in other words, often the best employees. Another method is to leave decisions about cutting up to the leaders of the agencies themselves. But as some veterans of Reinventing Government learned, that can have the effect of simply consolidating inertia in the managerial ranks. "Headquarters isn't ever gonna cut itself," says John Kamensky. "Headquarters cuts field."

The Need for Increases in the Workforce

Ideally, the White House ought to be able to keep agencies from playing such games. But just as agencies lack the manpower and expertise to oversee their contractors, the White House strains to oversee the rest of government. The Office of Management and Budget [OMB] is meant to be the eyes and ears of the executive branch. But with its staff of about 500, it is simply incapable of knowing what's working and what's not out in the labyrinths of the federal bureaucracy.

The paradox, then, is this: if the aim is to reform the civil service in order to put a lid on federal spending, what we really need are targeted increases in the federal workforce. A wise first move would be to double the size of the OMB. More and better staff at revenue-producing agencies like the IRS [Internal Revenue

Service] would also make sense. The SEC will need a big boost in personnel in order to fulfill the new demands of last year's financial reform legislation, which wisely calls for the agency to oversee derivatives trading and other potentially destabilizing aspects of the financial world. And our best hope for controlling the burgeoning costs of Medicare and Medicaid—the biggest drivers of long-term federal deficits—lies in new, yet-to-be staffed bureaucracies whose founding is authorized in last year's health care reform law.

But of course, Republicans have not only vowed to block funding for the financial and health reform laws, they're also making demands to cut the federal workforce by as much as 15 percent—all in the spirit of so-called fiscal responsibility. "The idea that we're somehow going to balance the budget by cutting the workforce is absurd," says John Palguta of the Partnership for Public Service. It's absurd for a number of reasons, but the biggest one is that, in today's government, cutting civil servants is bound to prove an exceedingly expensive way to be thrifty.

VIEWPOINT 3

> *"The level of government that has shown itself least capable of disciplining growth in healthcare has been assigned an even greater responsibility for this task going forward."*

The New Health Care Law Worsens Inefficiencies in Spending

Christopher J. Conover

In the following viewpoint, Christopher J. Conover argues that the Patient Protection and Affordable Care Act is going to worsen health spending inefficiencies. The author claims that under the new law, government spending on health is likely to increase, and the proposed mechanisms for controlling costs are not going to work. Conover argues that having government take responsibility for disciplining growth in costs, rather than the private sector, is a mistake. Conover is a research scholar in the Center for Health Policy and Inequalities Research at Duke University and an adjunct scholar at the American Enterprise Institute (AEI).

As you read, consider the following questions:

1. According to Conover, how many times larger was publicly financed health spending in 2007 compared with 1965?
2. The author claims that the share of the economy absorbed by mandatory federal health programs in 2035 will be what percent higher than in 2011?
3. Each incremental dollar of federal taxes is likely generating deadweight losses amounting to what, according to Conover?

The country is currently engaged in a pitched battle over the size of government, and the fierce struggle over the debt ceiling is a skirmish in this much larger war. Health spending is central to this debate. But many Americans may not realize the degree to which healthcare has dominated the growth of government over time. Between 1966 and 2007, the entire increase in the size of government relative to the economy resulted from growth in tax-financed health spending. . . .

Government Health Spending

As a share of GDP [gross domestic product], publicly financed health spending in 2007 was five times as large as it was in 1965 (the year immediately before Medicare and Medicaid began). In contrast, the share of the economy attributable to government spending on all other activities unrelated to health was identical in 1966 and 2007.

When 2007 is compared to 1966, the entire amount of the increase in the size of government between those years was accounted for by rising public expenditures on healthcare. Much of this, of course, was related to the rapid growth in Medicare and Medicaid spending.

The rise in government-funded healthcare has been extraordinary by any measure. In terms of constant purchasing power for everyday goods, tax-financed healthcare has increased 30-fold just since 1960. This includes all federal, state, and local government spending for healthcare, such as public health, direct delivery of health services, public health insurance, and investments in medical R&D [research and development] and facilities construction.

However, real federal spending on healthcare grew far faster than tax-paid healthcare overall. This reflects a substantial shift in the relative roles of federal government vis-à-vis state and local governments in financing (and regulating) healthcare. This shift will increase under the new healthcare law [the Patient Protection and Affordable Care Act].

In per capita terms, the overall increase was 17-fold. This does not mean that real per capita health output funded by taxpayers rose 17-fold in 50 years. . . . The increase represents how much more real output in the general economy was foregone to bankroll the tax-financed share of U.S. health spending in 2007 relative to 1966. This rapid increase in government health spending was approximately five times as large as the increase in overall government spending per person during the same time.

The tax-financed health share of the economy has risen every single year since 1929. Driven by continued growth in Medicaid and Medicare, that pattern was projected by the Congressional Budget Office [CBO] to continue over the next 75 years even before President [Barack] Obama was sworn into office. Unfortunately, rather than reverse this trend, the president devoted a considerable amount of political capital in his first 15 months in office to securing the enactment of a law that will accelerate its growth.

A Realistic Spending Scenario

The latest CBO figures show that under current law—i.e. assuming that everything works as planned under the new healthcare law—the share of GDP devoted to federal spending on mandatory health programs (Medicare and Medicaid) will be 68 percent higher in 2035 compared to 2011. But the CBO recognizes that certain components of the law intended to slow the growth in health costs may not work as planned. Under an alternative, more realistic scenario, the share of the economy absorbed by mandatory federal health programs will be 84 percent higher than this year [2011].

Why is this alternative scenario more realistic? One good reason is that for nearly a decade, Congress has refused to follow its own law to hold down physician spending. In 1997, Congress adopted a "sustainable growth rate" (SGR) formula to ensure that physician payments under Medicare grew at a reasonable rate. This resulted in a 4.8 percent cut in physician fees in 2002, but that was the only year the formula worked as designed. Since then, the same formula has called for continued cuts in physician fees to offset the ever-rising volume of physician services billed to Medicare.

From 2003 forward, however, Congress has on 13 different occasions taken legislative actions to prevent these fee reductions from being adopted. The latest such fix was signed into law last December and runs through the end of this year. Consequently, a series of small fee reductions now has accumulated to a statutorily required 29.5 percent cut in Medicare physician fees that will be needed for calendar year 2012 to remain in compliance with SGR.

Not surprisingly, such an enormous cut is being resisted by physicians, and, not surprisingly, Congress is likely to continue kicking this can down the road. After all, its own panel of experts—the Medicare Payment Advisory Commission (MedPAC)—concedes that "fee cuts of that magnitude would be detrimental to beneficiary access to care."

Yet the fee reductions implied by the Patient Protection and Affordable Care Act would, by 2085, result in Medicare physician fees being 70 percent lower than the fees paid by private health insurers. Yet the current law projections done by CBO *require* them to assume that such cuts take place, since that is what the statute now on the books mandates until and unless Congress again enacts another temporary statutory fix to avert this. CBO's alternative scenario more sensibly concludes these cuts are unlikely to happen; hence Medicare spending will be higher.

The Projected Impact of IPAB

Another mechanism that CBO has concluded may not work is the Independent Payment Advisory Board (IPAB). Under the new healthcare law, IPAB will be required to submit proposals to reduce Medicare's spending per enrollee if the growth in such spending is projected to exceed specified targets.

Why is IPAB needed? In the words of one proponent: "A common theme in the healthcare reform debate in recent years has been the need for a board of impartial experts to oversee the healthcare system. . . . Congress is too driven by special-interest politics and too limited in expertise and vision to control costs."

To circumvent this reality, IPAB's recommendations (in contrast to MedPAC's, which are purely advisory) would go into effect *automatically* unless (as the CBO puts it) they are "blocked or replaced by subsequent legislative action." Sound familiar? IPAB will work so long as Congress—an institution driven by special-interest politics—doesn't do to IPAB what it already has done repeatedly with the SGR.

What's interesting is that CBO projects in their baseline scenario that under current law, growth in Medicare spending will remain below IPAB's target growth rate over the next decade. In short, IPAB will have nothing to do because nothing will trigger the need for it to take action.

But in their alternative fiscal scenario, CBO further assumes IPAB will be "difficult to sustain" and therefore would not continue past 2021. Bottom line: in their more realistic scenario (one that accounts for the actual past behavior of Congress, not just its good intentions), CBO has implicitly assumed that IPAB will have *zero* impact on spending either in the short term or long term.

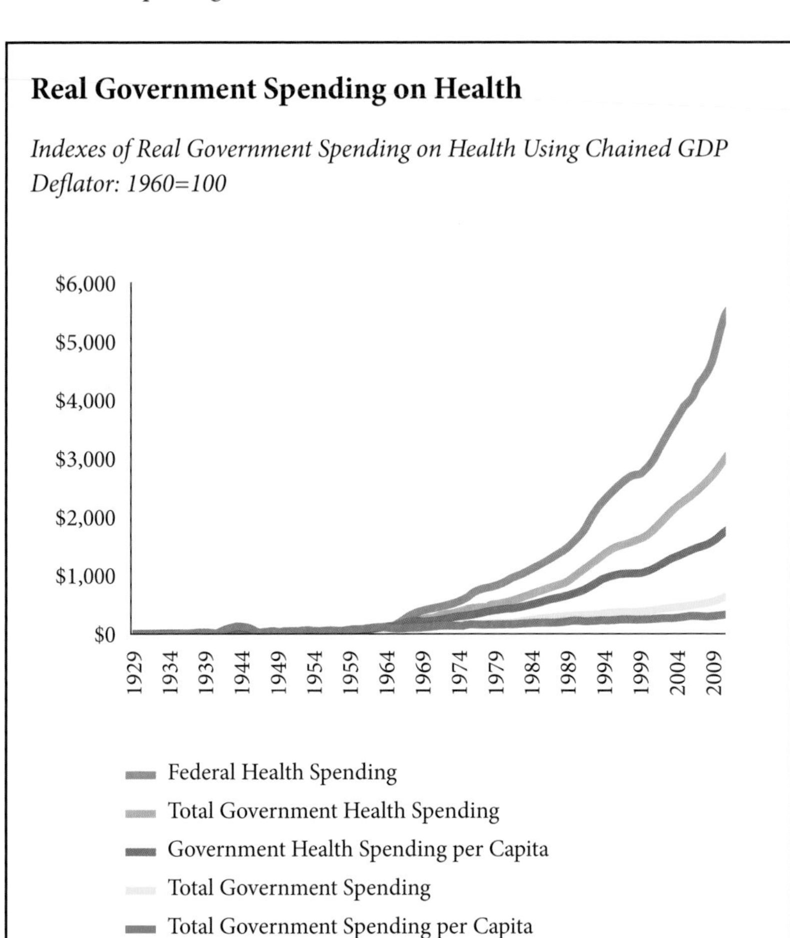

TAKEN FROM: Christopher J. Conover, "Health Is the Health of the State," *American*, July 19, 2011. www.american.com.

The Cost Growth for Medicare

The third Medicare policy that might be difficult to sustain over a long period, in CBO's estimation, is tying increases in payment rates to increases in productivity in the general economy. Once again, this provision flies in the face of historical experience, which shows that hospital productivity growth was "small or negligible" from 1981 to 2005. Even Medicare's own actuary has stated these "are unlikely to be sustainable on a permanent annual basis." Roughly 15 percent of Medicare Part A providers (hospitals, skilled nursing facilities, home health agencies, and hospice providers) would become unprofitable within the first decade if these productivity adjustments were adopted as scheduled by law. By 2065, these rules would result in Medicare and Medicaid payments for hospital inpatient services falling to 60 percent below the amounts paid by private health insurers. Who can possibly believe this would ever happen?

CBO's well-warranted pessimism regarding the ability of government to control Medicare spending extends even further. CBO makes its projections of long-term health spending based on assumptions about "excess cost growth." Excess cost growth is the annual increase in healthcare spending per person relative to growth in GDP per person after controlling for the effects of demographic changes on healthcare spending, such as changes in the age distribution of those eligible for Medicare, Medicaid, and private insurance.

Historically (from 1975 to 2007), Medicare's excess cost growth has been 2.4 percent, compared to only 2.0 percent for Medicaid and 1.9 percent for all other (i.e., predominantly private) health spending.

These figures may seem small and the difference between them even smaller. But the excess cost growth for Medicare implies that the program doubles as a share of the economy every 29 years, whereas for the private health sector, that doubling period is every 37 years.

But CBO argues that "healthcare expenditures cannot rise more quickly than GDP per capita forever." Consequently, CBO analysts assume that pressures to hold down costs will result in excess cost growth for Medicaid and private health insurance premiums being driven to 0 percent in 2085.

In contrast, it assumes that excess cost growth in Medicare will decline from 1.7 percentage points in 2022 to 1.0 percent in 2085. Why the difference? Well, as CBO concedes, "in the absence of changes in federal law, state governments and the private sector have more flexibility to respond to the pressures of rising healthcare spending than does the federal government."

The Impact of Government-Funded Healthcare

Of course, all of the figures understate the true impact of tax-financed healthcare on the economy. Every dollar of taxes imposes hidden costs on the economy in the form of lower output (also called "deadweight losses"). That is, we get less of whatever we tax, be it labor, commodities, or even health services.

At the margin, each incremental dollar of federal taxes is likely generating deadweight losses amounting to 44 cents on the dollar. Thus, unless one can make the case that tax-financed healthcare is 44 percent more efficient than the same dollar raised and spent privately, every dollar we shift away from the private sector onto the books of government is a losing proposition.

With that in mind, it is difficult to justify using tax dollars to bankroll Medicare for people like [billionaire] Warren Buffett, or to retain a system of tax subsidies for private health insurance that provides a much larger subsidy (dollarwise and as a percent of premium) to [billionaire] Bill Gates than a low-income laborer.

But rather than fix the pervasive inefficiencies or inequities created by tax-financed healthcare, the Obama health plan has amplified both. The level of government that has shown itself least capable of disciplining growth in healthcare has been assigned an even greater responsibility for this task going forward.

And instead of eradicating the upside-down subsidies endemic in the tax exclusion for employer-provided coverage, the new health plan not only retains these, but will create even more massive inequities by offering a worker lucky enough to get coverage through health exchanges literally thousands of dollars more in subsidies than if that identical worker remains stuck in an employer-based health plan. To paraphrase Ronald Reagan, "government-funded healthcare isn't the solution to the problem: it is the problem." When will we ever learn?

Viewpoint 4

> *"A major goal of the health reform measure is to push against higher spending while simultaneously promoting higher quality care."*

Repealing the New Health Care Law Would Increase Wasteful Spending

Jonathan Cohn

In the following viewpoint, Jonathan Cohn argues that calls for repealing the Patient Protection and Affordable Care Act are politically motivated and misguided. Cohn claims that Republican criticism of the act based on a belief in eliminating government waste is incompatible with the criticism of the act's reduction in Medicare spending. In fact, Cohn argues, the act will rein in health care costs by eliminating unnecessary Medicare spending. Cohn is a senior editor at The New Republic *and author of* Sick: The Untold Story of America's Health Care Crisis—and the People Who Pay the Price.

As you read, consider the following questions:

1. According to the author, the Affordable Care Act will reduce spending on Medicare by how much over the next ten years?

2. Cohn claims that repeated independent studies have come to what conclusion about government payments through Medicare?
3. What alternative to the Affordable Care Act proposed by Republican Representative Paul Ryan does the author argue is more honest?

Suppose I told you one of the political parties was determined to increase wasteful government spending by hundreds of billions of dollars, to pay the salaries of countless extra bureaucrats and to degrade the quality of medicine in the U.S. If you've been paying attention to politics for the last few months, you'd probably assume I was talking about the Democrats. Not so. I'd actually be talking about the Republicans who want to repeal health care reform.

The Republican Arguments for Repeal

Confused? Well, don't blame yourself. The Republicans and their allies have spent a lot of time—and a *lot* of money—attacking the Affordable Care Act and promising to undo it. And they have done so with such a fury that almost nobody seemed to notice they are making a pair of arguments that are fundamentally incompatible.

The Republicans start their calls for repeal with a familiar, thematic critique of government. The new health law, in this telling, represents an unconscionable government intrusion into the private sector and, ultimately, an encroachment on individual liberty. The federal government will be dictating everything from how employers conduct their businesses to how doctors treat their patients. And, oh yes, the government will be spending a ton of money it does not now have, increasing the deficit and/or laying new burdens on the taxpayers. The argument is hyperbolic and, in places, downright inaccurate. But, at least, it is consistent with longtime conservative principles about the role and size of government.

But that's not all the Republicans have been arguing. They've also been attacking the health overhaul for what it will do to Medicare. And instead of accusing Democrats of trying to dump more money into a government program, as Republicans would typically do, they've attacked Democrats for doing the very opposite—noting that the Affordable Care Act will reduce spending on Medicare somewhere around $400 billion over the next ten years. Apparently government-run health care is awful, except, um, when it isn't.

The Waste in Medicare

To be fair, the Republican argument makes perfect sense if you think like a campaign operative. Senior citizens are, at the moment, the most conservative age group in the electorate. They were least likely to support President [Barack] Obama in 2008 and, during the health care fight, were most likely to oppose enactment. Republicans seized on that fact and have gleefully proclaimed themselves champions of Medicare, despite a long history of opposing it and, as Newt Gingrich once put it, letting this universal social insurance program "wither on the vine." Seniors are playing along, since they figure reform means taking money once targeted for Medicare and diverting it to help people under-65 pay for their medical care.

But here's where things could get complicated for the advocates of repeal. Consider what undoing the cuts in Medicare would entail. It would start, first of all, with restoring higher payments to the insurers that provide private coverage for people in Medicare, through what's known as the Medicare Advantage plans. There's a reason the health law reduces those payments: Repeated independent studies, including those by the well-respected Medicare Payment Advisory Commission, determined that the government was paying the insurers too much.

Restore those payments, and you're wasting taxpayer dollars. And a lot of those wasted dollars will go to hiring new people to work at insurance companies. They won't be government bureau-

Seniors and the Affordable Care Act

When Democrats in Congress finally passed health-reform legislation in 2010, they did so without the support of seniors. The Affordable Care Act was not socialized medicine; it was an effort to fill in the holes of the existing insurance system with a minimum of disruption to established institutions and the protected public. But much of the protected public could never be won over to a program that they perceived as primarily benefiting the poor and minorities. No age group objected to the Affordable Care Act more than the elderly. Indeed, in some polls, they were the only age group against the law; a Gallup poll in June 2010 found 60 percent of seniors saying the adoption of reform was a "bad thing," while 57 percent of 18- to 29-year-olds and a plurality of other age groups said it was a "good thing"

Paul Starr, "The Medicare Bind,"
American Prospect, *October 12, 2011.*

crats, obviously. They'll be insurance company bureaucrats. But is that really better? Is the Tea Party in favor of waste as long as it lines the pockets of insurance executives rather than Uncle Sam?

The New Health Law

Meanwhile, restoring the other cuts to Medicare would mean rescinding payment reductions designed to make the program more efficient. Remember, a major goal of the health reform measure is to push against higher spending while simultaneously promoting higher quality care. In the case of Medicare, that means slowing down payment increases to providers and penalizing those that provide substandard treatment; while, at the same time, boosting payments to primary care doctors and providing bonuses for those who actually treat patients better.

Reasonable people can argue how well these efforts will work. But allowing Medicare to continue going along as it has been for the last ten to twenty years—which is what repealing the new health law would do—would almost surely force a choice between much higher taxes or much worse access to care. If you don't believe me, just look at the plan proposed by Republican Representative Paul Ryan, who is forthright enough to admit that the GOP alternative to the Democrats' approach to Medicare is to reduce radically its guaranteed benefits.

Of course, the Republican Party's leadership hasn't embraced Ryan's plan in any specificity. And, at least for the short term, it seems unlikely they'll advocate such a path, lest they scare off the seniors that just handed them control of the House of Representatives. But that means Republicans are now on the side of wasting taxpayer dollars on a government program that, in fact, needs some reform. I wonder how long it will be until the Tea Party figures that out.

> *"Only when we make meaningful investments in schools—not prisons—will our nation reap the benefits."*

Education vs. Incarceration

Steven Hawkins

In the following viewpoint, Steven Hawkins argues that funding priorities need to change to increase investment in schools and decrease spending on imprisonment. Hawkins argues that over the last few decades, spending on incarceration has increased, while spending on education has decreased. Hawkins claims that the grim effect of current spending priorities is clear in urban neighborhoods around the country that have poor schools and high incarceration rates. Hawkins is executive vice president and chief program officer of the National Association for the Advancement of Colored People (NAACP).

As you read, consider the following questions:

1. According to the author, what percent of imprisonment spending happens at the state level?
2. Hawkins claims that what percent of low-performing schools in Los Angeles are in neighborhoods with the highest incarceration rates?

Steven Hawkins, "Education vs. Incarceration," *American Prospect*, vol. 22, no. 1, December 6, 2010.

3. What six benefits does the author claim would come from making meaningful investments in schools?

More money must go to schools than to prisons before high-crime neighborhoods can truly be reformed.

Since 1980, the U.S. prison population has grown exponentially, expanding from approximately 500,000 to 2.3 million people in just three decades. America now has the dubious distinction of leading the world in prison population: We account for 25 percent of all prisoners but only 5 percent of the global population. Our penchant for punishment has come at a cost. We spend almost $70 billion annually to place adults in prison and jails, to confine youth in detention centers, and to supervise 7.3 million individuals on probation and parole. Indeed, confinement costs have claimed an increasing share of state and local government spending. This trend has starved essential social programs—most notably education.

Nearly 75 percent of imprisonment spending happens at the state level, where dollars are drawn from a general fund that is meant to pay for a range of public needs, including health care, housing, public assistance, and education. Whether we look back over the last two decades, or just the last two years, education, in particular, has become a casualty of state budget battles. Analysis by the National Association of State Budget Officers shows that elementary and high schools receive 73 percent of their state funding from this discretionary fund; colleges and universities count on the fund for half of their budgets. However, $9 out of every $10 that support imprisonment come from the same pot of money. With tens of billions of dollars in prison spending annually, states are finding that there is simply less discretionary money available to invest in education, especially in these lean economic times.

Indeed, as the economic downturn limited all state spending in the fiscal year 2008–2009, the share of general-fund

Prison Spending and Higher Education Funding

Over the last few years, the budget battle between prisons and universities for state discretionary dollars has been won by prisons in virtually every state in the county. In 2008, the Pew Center on the States looked back at state spending patterns between 1987 and 2007 and found that after adjusting for inflation, funding for higher education grew by a modest 21 percent, while corrections funding grew by 127 percent, six times the rate of higher education.

National Association for the Advancement of Colored People, "Misplaced Priorities: Over Incarcerate, Under Educate," April 2011. www.naacp.org.

money going to incarceration grew as expenditures in every other category—save public assistance—declined. States still spend more of their general-fund dollars on education than on incarceration, but the percentage of dollars being used for incarceration is increasing, while the percentage for education is decreasing. In 33 of 50 states, corrections-related costs made up a larger proportion of the general fund than in the previous fiscal year, while spending on K–12 and higher education decreased.

The federal stimulus, no doubt, helped states find money to pay for both prisons and other basic state services as tax revenue eroded. When future budget years arrive, however, and states and counties try to balance their books without the assistance of the federal stimulus, young people will experience more of the same: school closings, teacher layoffs, diminished after-school programs, and rising tuition at colleges and universities. All of this will happen while prison spending grows.

This tradeoff between education and incarceration is particularly acute at the community level. In many urban neighborhoods where millions of dollars are spent to lock up residents, the education infrastructure is crippled. As the prison population skyrocketed in the past three decades, researchers began to notice that high concentrations of inmates were coming from a few select neighborhoods—primarily poor communities of color—in major cities. These were dubbed "million-dollar blocks" to reflect that spending on incarceration was the predominant public-sector investment in these neighborhoods. NAACP research shows that matching zip codes to high rates of incarceration also reveals where low-performing schools, as measured by math proficiency, tend to cluster. The lowest-performing schools tend to be in the areas where incarceration rates are the highest. The following examples are instructive.

Los Angeles. California has the largest prison population in the country, with more than 170,000 individuals behind bars. In Los Angeles, more than half of current parolees live in neighborhoods that are home to less than 20 percent of the city's adult residents. More than a billion dollars are spent every year to incarcerate people from these communities. At the same time, as of spring 2010, the Los Angeles Unified School District was projecting a deficit of $640 million in the 2010–11 academic year. As a result, district officials were planning to raise class sizes and lay off thousands of teachers and other school-based staff.

How is school success affected by these policy choices and spending patterns? There is no definitive way to know what the previous spending cuts have meant for Los Angeles schools, but we do know that in Los Angeles, 67 percent of low-performing schools are in neighborhoods with the highest incarceration rates. By contrast, 68 percent of the city's high-performing schools are in neighborhoods with the lowest incarceration rates.

Philadelphia. In 2009, the School District of Philadelphia faced a projected budget shortfall of $147 million, after losing $160 million in state funding. Yet, during this same period, taxpayers spent nearly $290 million to imprison residents from just 11 Philadelphia neighborhoods, home to about one-quarter of the city's population.

As hundreds of millions of dollars are invested in incarcerating people from these select neighborhoods, the corresponding disinvestment in education in those neighborhoods is telling. Sixty-six percent of lower-performing schools are clustered in or very near neighborhoods with the highest rates of incarceration—where the biggest taxpayer investment in imprisonment is being made. By contrast, 75 percent of Philadelphia's higher-performing schools are in neighborhoods with the lowest rates of incarceration.

Houston. In the 2009–2010 academic year, state budget cuts forced the Houston Independent School District to manage a projected $10 million shortfall. However, in the preceding year, Texas spent over $175 million to imprison residents from just 10 neighborhoods in Houston. In Houston, of the six schools deemed lower-performing, five are in neighborhoods with the highest rates of incarceration. By contrast, of the 12 schools considered higher-performing, eight are in neighborhoods with the lowest incarceration rates.

What we learn from Los Angeles, Houston, and Philadelphia is that our national priorities are misplaced, and with devastating consequences. In a few select neighborhoods, the heavy investment in incarceration over education correlates with the lowest-performing schools. These neighborhoods send more individuals to prison than to college—reflecting the pattern of dollars invested. The relationship has not yet been shown to be causal, but we do see a correlative effect between education and incarceration. If states were to properly invest in reopening schools, keeping quality teachers, maintaining sensible classroom sizes, and sustaining the affordability of higher education, it's quite possible—particularly for economic crimes like low-level drug dealing—we would not need to imprison so many people and could stop sinking our valuable taxpayer dollars into an investment that has demonstrated scant return.

To shift our funding priorities, national and state policymakers will have to choose cost-effective criminal-justice policies and focus on public-safety strategies that curb crime and reserve more of our tax dollars for our children's education. Gov. Arnold Schwarzenegger of California noted in his 2010 State of the State address: "Spending 45 percent more on prisons than universities is no way to proceed into the future. . . . What does it say about any state that focuses more on prison uniforms than on caps and gowns?" Only when we make meaningful investments in schools—not prisons will our nation reap the benefits through increased earnings for families, reduced unemployment, increased tax revenues from more vibrant local economies, reduced reliance on public assistance, increased civic engagement, and improved public safety outcomes for neighborhoods at risk of violence and victimization.

> *"While Washington spends huge sums on things that are education-related, the riches produce almost nothing of educational value."*

Spending on Education Should Be Reduced

Neal McCluskey

In the following viewpoint, Neal McCluskey argues that the federal government's increased spending on education is not producing results and should be reduced. McCluskey claims that increased education spending over the last few decades has yielded more school employees, student aid, and political power for education, but little in terms of learning outcomes. McCluskey is associate director of the Cato Institute's Center for Educational Freedom and author of Feds in the Classroom: How Big Government Corrupts, Cripples, and Compromises American Education.

As you read, consider the following questions:

1. By how many dollars did federal spending per student increase from 1970 to 2006, according to McCluskey?
2. According to the author, how much did average math scores improve from 1973 to 2008?

Neal McCluskey, "For the Nation's Sake, Cut Education Spending," *Daily Caller*, January 25, 2011. http://dailycaller.com.

3. McCluskey says that the federal government spends how many billion dollars a year on K–12 education and higher education?

If President [Barack] Obama cares about restoring sanity to federal finances, he will demand deep cuts to education spending. That's right: In tonight's State of the Union address [January 25, 2011], he will call to axe most of Washington's educationally worthless outlays.

Unfortunately, Mr. Obama is likely to prove that he doesn't care all that much about attacking the nation's crushing debt. According to several sources, he'll not only place education spending off limits, he might make increasing it a focal point of tonight's address.

But wait: Debt or no debt, isn't having an educated citizenry crucial to the nation's future? Isn't he right to protect education funding?

The Increase in Education Spending

Education is, indeed, very important. But while Washington spends huge sums on things that are education-related, the riches produce almost nothing of educational value. If anything, the feds keep stuffing donuts into an already obese system.

Federal elementary and secondary education spending has risen mightily since the early 1970s, when Washington first started immersing itself in education. In 1970, according to the federal *Digest of Education Statistics*, Uncle Sam spent an inflation-adjusted $31.5 billion on public K–12 education. By 2009 that had ballooned to $82.9 billion.

On a per-pupil basis, in 1970 the feds spent $435 per student. By 2006—the latest year with available data—it was $1,015, a 133 percent increase. And it's not like state and local spending was dropping: Real, overall, per-pupil spending rose from $5,593 in 1970 to $12,463 in 2006, and today we beat almost every other industrialized nation in education funding.

US Education Spending

While students in many developed nations have been learning more and more over time, American 15-year-olds are stuck in the middle of the pack in many fundamental areas, including reading and math. Yet the United States is near the top in education spending.

Veronique de Rugy, "Losing the Brains Race," Reason, *March 2011.*

The Impact of More Spending

What do we have to show for this?

Certainly more public school employees: Between 1969 and 2007, pupil-to-staff ratios were close to halved. Not coincidentally, these same people politick powerfully for ever more spending and against reforms that will challenge their bloated monopoly. They also routinely defeat efforts to hold them accountable for results.

This constant feeding of special interests is why we've gotten zilch in the outcome that really matters—learning. Since the early 1970s, scores on the National Assessment of Educational Progress—the "Nation's Report Card"—have been utterly stagnant for 17-year-olds, our schools' "final products." In 1973 the average math score was 304 (out of 500). In 2008 it was just 306. In reading, the 1971 average was 285. In 2008 it was up a single point, hitting 286.

The higher education tale is much the same, especially for student aid, the primary college dumping ground for federal dollars. According to the College Board, in 1971 Washington provided $3,814 in inflation-adjusted aid per full-time equivalent student. By 2009–10 that figure had more than tripled, hitting $12,894.

By most available indicators this has been money down the drain. For instance, only about 58 percent of bachelor's seekers finish their programs within six years, if at all. Literacy levels among people with degrees are low and falling. And colleges have raised their prices at astronomical rates to capture ever-growing aid.

An Expensive Political Issue

What's the total damage?

It's impossible to know exactly because so many federal programs touch on education, but the *Digest* provides a decent estimate. In the 2008–09 academic year, Washington spent roughly $83 billion on K–12 education and $37 billion on higher education. (The latter, notably, excludes student-loan funds that fuel the tuition skyrocket but generally get repaid, as well as federally funded research conducted at universities.) Add those together and you get $120 billion, a sum that's doing no educational good and, therefore, leaves no excuse for not applying it to our $14 trillion debt.

And yet, it seems President Obama will not only protect education spending, he might fight to increase it. Why?

He could certainly believe that huge spending on education is a good thing. That, though, might mean he hasn't looked at all at what we've gotten for our money.

Unfortunately, it might also be that education is the easiest of all issues through which to buy political capital, whether from special interests like teachers' unions, or busy parents who don't have time to research what education funds actually produce. It's also ideal for demonizing opponents who might demand discomfiting fiscal discipline.

Of course, misguided intentions and political exploitation have been at work for decades in education, so this isn't new. We are now well past the point where we can ignore results. Today, we simply cannot afford to keep throwing money away.

Periodical and Internet Sources Bibliography

The following articles have been selected to supplement the diverse views presented in this chapter.

Andrew G. Biggs	"Why Does Government Grow and Grow and Grow?," *The American*, September 16, 2010.
Veronique de Rugy	"Does ObamaCare Reduce Health Care Spending?," Reason.com, November 4, 2010.
Jeffrey Keefe	"Debunking the Myth of the Overcompensated Public Employee: The Evidence," EPI Briefing Paper No. 276, September 15, 2010.
Ronald Kessler	"The Real Problem with Government Spending," *Newsmax*, March 4, 2011.
Edward D. Kleinbard	"The Hidden Hand of Government Spending," *Regulation*, Fall 2010.
Steven Mufson	"Before Solyndra, a Long History of Failed Government Energy Projects," *Washington Post*, November 11, 2011.
Peter Orszag	"To Save Money, Save the Health Care Act," *New York Times*, November 3, 2010.
Robert Pollin and Jeffrey Thompson	"The Betrayal of Public Workers," *Nation*, February 16, 2011.
John Schmitt	"The Wage Penalty for State and Local Government Employees," Center for Economic and Policy Research, May 2010. www.cepr.net.
Weekly Standard	"Green Jobs in the Red," September 12, 2011.

Chapter 2

Should Government Spending Allow Deficits and Debt?

Chapter Preface

In August 2011, Standard & Poor's ratings services downgraded the US government's long-term sovereign credit rating from AAA to AA+. The financial services company said, "Our lowering of the rating was prompted by our view on the rising public debt burden and our perception of greater policymaking uncertainty." The announcement fueled the fire to an already tendentious debate in the United States about deficit spending and the rising public debt. Government deficit spending is nothing new, but concerns have been raised because of the rate of increase in deficit spending and the failure of government to come to an agreement about how to deal with the growing debt in the future.

The United States has been in debt since its founding, running annual deficits for almost every year. Deficit spending refers to the annual spending that the government makes beyond what it collects in revenues. Occasionally, the government will take in more money than it spends, which is known as a surplus. The federal government had surpluses most recently during the four fiscal years from 1998 to 2001. Although surplus years may shrink the debt, they will not necessarily eliminate it. The national public debt refers to the cumulative amount of money the government owes to investors—which can include banks, private investors, and foreign governments—and to US government trust funds.

According to the US Department of the Treasury, as of April 2012 the total national public debt was more than $15.6 trillion, with more than $10.8 trillion of debt held by investors and more than $4.7 trillion in intergovernmental holdings. In fiscal year 2011 alone, the total debt grew by more than $1 trillion. In the decade from April 2002 to April 2012, the total public debt increased by more than $9.6 trillion. Congress has the ability to determine an aggregate limit for debt, but with more than a dozen increases in the past decade, the ceiling appears to be quite impermanent and likely to be raised when needed.

There is wide disagreement about whether current deficit spending and increases in the public debt are big problems. Where there is agreement, however, is that although the current levels of deficit spending and debt accumulation cannot go on forever, it is far easier for government to agree to fund new programs or tax cuts than it is for government to agree on cuts in spending. The authors of the viewpoints in this chapter discuss annual deficit spending and offer a variety of proposed solutions.

VIEWPOINT 1

"The only way to fix this mess is to radically cut federal spending, cap the budget with pay-as-you-go spending rules, and then enact a balanced budget amendment."

The United States Should Adopt a Balanced Budget Amendment

Steven G. Calabresi

In the following viewpoint, Steven G. Calabresi argues that the solution to the growing US debt is a balanced budget amendment (BBA). Calabresi claims that the only way to effectively cut spending is to make overspending unconstitutional. He contends that a BBA will have many positive effects, such as lowering risks for investment in the United States and improving national security. Calabresi is a professor of law at Northwestern University Law School and chairman of the board of the Federalist Society for Law and Public Policy Studies.

As you read, consider the following questions:

1. According to the author, the US federal debt totaled what amount at the writing of this viewpoint?

Steven G. Calabresi, "The Answer Is a Balanced Budget Amendment," *American Spectator*, October 2011. http://spectator.org.

2. Calabresi claims that Congress borrows what portion of every dollar it spends?
3. The author claims that US global power is threatened due to the fact that approximately what fraction of current levels of deficit spending is financed by foreign countries?

The United States of America is on the road to bankruptcy, with a federal debt of more than $14.2 trillion, almost half of which is owned by foreign countries. (Communist China alone owns fully a quarter of the foreign-held portion). The problem is so well known that it almost came as an anticlimax when Standard & Poor's recently downgraded U.S. debt from its coveted AAA rating to an unheard-of AA+. As for the budget deficit, it is expected to total $1.3 trillion for this year [2011] alone, with tax revenues of about $2.3 trillion and total expenditures of about $3.6 trillion. If a household ran its budget like that, we would say it was headed for a rude shock.

Making matters worse is that our debt is structural rather than cyclical: the federal budget is in deficit both in good economic times and bad. When George W. Bush took office in 2001, the gross federal debt was $5.76 trillion. When he left eight years later, the debt was up to $10.626 trillion, an increase of $607 billion a year. During Barack Obama's presidency it has risen by $1.7 trillion a year and now almost 40 percent higher than when he took office. Deficits of this size are quite simply unsustainable.

A Proposed Fix

The only way to fix this mess is to radically cut federal spending, cap the budget with pay-as-you-go spending rules, and then enact a balanced budget amendment (BBA).

The most important point is that we need to cut spending, not raise taxes. Total federal spending as a percentage of Gross Domestic Product (GDP) has skyrocketed from around 18 percent, when George W. Bush became president, to more than 25 percent today. This shows that our current deficit problem is entirely due to *overspending*. If tomorrow we cut spending back to the levels of January 20, 2001, when Bush took office, the deficit would almost disappear.

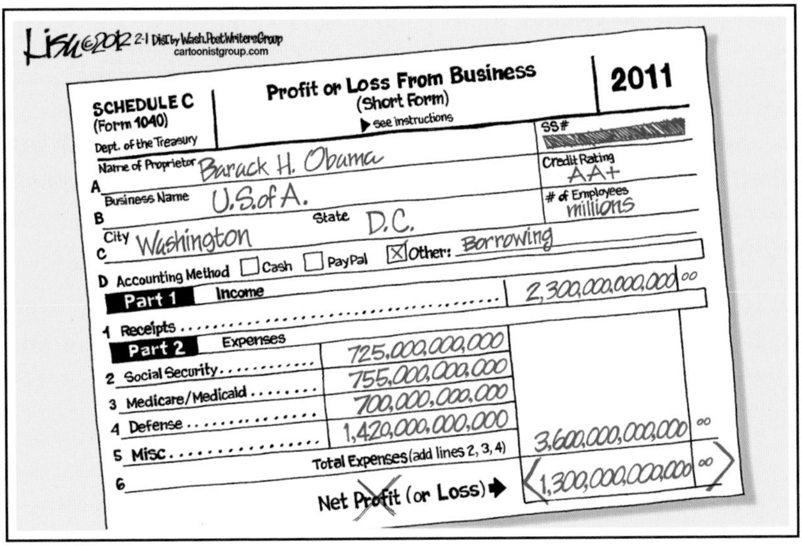

Then we need to cap and balance the budget, once we've cut overall spending back to 2001 levels. To do this effectively, we need to enact a federal BBA to the U.S. Constitution. This amendment should have several features.

First, it should require that the president submit to Congress each year a balanced federal budget with no fiscal gimmicks. Presidential failure to do so would be an impeachable offense. Congress should be constitutionally required to hold a vote in both houses on the president's proposed budget within three months, with the president and Congress having up to six months to adopt a final budget in any given calendar year (this requirement should be waivable during any time of declared war for up to two years). If they fail to do that, all federal spending except for payments on the debt should be frozen at levels 10 percent lower than in the preceding fiscal year. To help impose this, any one of the several states should have standing to sue in the Supreme Court's original jurisdiction for enforcement of this requirement.

Second, the BBA should cap federal spending at 18 percent of GDP. A spending cap of this proportion would keep the federal government at the size it was under President Bill Clinton—hardly onerous or severe. The amendment should require a two-thirds vote of both houses of Congress to enact any new taxes or to raise tax rates. Votes to raise the national debt limit should also require a two-thirds majority. These provisions are essential to prevent a BBA from becoming just an excuse to raise taxes.

The Need for Constitutional Protection

The usual response to calls for such an amendment is that we ought not tamper with the Constitution. Critics of a BBA also claim it is not needed since a majority of Congress could balance the budget today if it really wanted to. There are at least five reasons why those critics are dead wrong.

First, it is a core principle of American constitutionalism that there be no taxation without representation. The American Revolution was fought in part to prevent taxation by a British Parliament in which Americans were not represented. When Congress borrows 40 cents of every dollar it spends, as it is doing today, it passes the burden of paying for current spending on to our children and grandchildren who cannot vote right now—nothing less than taxation without representation.

Second, a core purpose of the Constitution is to protect fundamental principles like freedom of speech and of the press from being whittled away during moments of legislative passion. Exactly the same argument holds true with respect to spending more money than the government collects in tax revenue. Constitutionalizing the balanced budget requirement is as necessary as constitutionalizing the protection of freedom of speech and of the press. This is an argument that was first made more than 30 years ago by Noble Prize laureate Milton Friedman. It is just as true today as it was then.

The Economic Justifications

Third, there is an economic reason why it is easier to assemble lobbies for government spending than it is to assemble a nationwide lobby for a balanced budget. Consider the farm lobby that argues for agricultural price supports, or the AARP [American Association of Retired Persons] that lobbies for benefits for the elderly. It is cheaper and easier for small groups with a shared common interest to lobby Congress than for a large, diffuse majority of the American population to do the same. That's why the silent majority is silent. A BBA in the Constitution would prevent the special interests from ripping off the children and grandchildren of the silent majority. James Madison wrote in *The Federalist No. 51* that the secret of constitutional government was to make ambition counteract ambition. The way to check and balance over-spending is to constitutionalize a pay-as-you-go rule while making tax increases hard to enact.

Fourth, yet another economic reason for a BBA is that it would reduce risk and thereby promote investment. When people are looking for a place to invest, one of their first questions is how risky is the investment and how large is the potential reward. Foreign and American investors since World War II have invested in the U.S. and in its debt because our Constitution of checks and balances makes it hard to do crazy things like nationalize industries or set up a single payer health insurance monopoly.

A BBA would reduce further the risk of investing in the U.S., and that would promote investment and economic growth by constitutionally committing itself not to overspend. The risk of inflationary devaluation of the dollar would thus go way down. This in turn would bolster the dollar as the world's reserve currency. It would also prevent federal borrowing from crowding out private sector borrowing in the U.S. This would free up a capital for investment in job-creating ventures.

The Symbolic Value

A fifth argument for the BBA paradoxically grows out of one of the arguments commonly made against it: it would be purely symbolic. Or as James Madison would have said, "a mere parchment barrier" against overspending.

This criticism fails for many reasons. A BBA of the kind I argue for would have enforcement teeth. Presidential failure to submit a good-faith balanced budget would be a specific ground for impeachment. Then too, if Congress failed to enact a balanced budget, state governments could sue for an across the board spending cut of 10 percent.

But suppose Congress wimps out and enacts a BBA without teeth. Would such a symbolic victory be worth anything? The answer again is clearly yes. Almost every state has some form of a balanced budget requirement in its constitution or law. The fact is that balanced budget requirements actually do work at the state level. This strongly suggests they would work at the federal level as well.

Constitutional provisions, even symbolic ones, set the agenda of political debate. The Second and Tenth Amendments clearly do that in the U.S. today, even though the federal courts almost never enforce them. A BBA would work very much the same way.

The case for a BBA is so powerful that Germany and Switzerland—both models of fiscal sobriety—actually require a balanced budget in their own constitutions. And now Germany and France have actually proposed requiring that all Eurozone countries amend their national constitutions to require a balanced budget. What is good enough for almost every state in the Union and for many countries of Europe is certainly worth trying at the federal level here.

The Concern About Taxes

So what harm could come from enacting a BBA to the U.S. Constitution? Is there any argument against such an amendment that outweighs the arguments in favor of it?

One concern conservatives have is that it might lead to tax increases. I share that concern and therefore would couple it with a super-majority requirement for tax increases. That should make a BBA clearly appealing to conservatives of all stripes. But what if such an amendment gets ratified that does not protect against tax increases? Would we then be worse off?

I think the answer is no. It is harder politically for Congress to tax real people living today than it is to borrow money from the children and grandchildren of the silent majority. People living today will mobilize in many ways against tax increases. The correct solution is to cut, cap, and balance, but I would not let concerns about tax increases stop us from doing what virtually every state constitution does.

The Future of the United States

Another real concern for conservatives is that a BBA could lead to dangerous cuts in spending on national defense. This concern I share. The U.S. is a world leader and the greatest force for liberty and economic opportunity in history. We must always be ready to defend liberty worldwide.

The problem is, however, that current levels of deficit spending—almost half of which is financed by foreign countries—is itself a threat to U.S. global might. We simply cannot defend liberty in Asia, for example, if we continue to borrow massively from the Chinese. We cannot defend freedom in Arab countries while being so dependent on Saudi Arabia and others for imported oil and purchases of our debt. The status quo is at least as threatening to America's military might as is living under a BBA, for the status quo is not sustainable.

Finally, some conservatives argue that the solution to congressional deficit spending is a line item veto amendment giving the president the same power over spending enjoyed by a majority of state governors. I am quite skeptical about such an amendment because of the enormous power it would shift from Congress to the president. Imagine for a moment that President

Obama could threaten senators or representatives with line item vetoes of locally important spending projects unless they voted his way on socialized medicine. Or on a card check law reform making it easy to fraudulently form a union. Do we really want to cede that much power from Congress to the president? I do not think so.

In sum, we need to cut, cap, and balance. To do that permanently, we must enact a BBA. Nothing less than the future of government of the people, by the people, and for the people is at stake.

"A strictly balanced budget is not important enough to be written into the Constitution."

The United States Should Not Adopt a Balanced Budget Amendment

Rich Lowry

In the following viewpoint, Rich Lowry argues that a balanced budget amendment is the wrong solution to controlling government deficit spending and reducing the debt. Lowry claims that it would be ineffective to alter the US Constitution in an attempt to balance the budget and would lead to lawsuits. Furthermore, he contends that proposed exceptions to the amendment would not adequately allow Congress to increase spending for necessary military expenses. Lowry is editor of the National Review *and a syndicated columnist.*

As you read, consider the following questions:

1. According to Lowry, in which decade did Congress last consider a balanced budget amendment?
2. The author compares a balanced budget amendment to what controversial amendment in US history?

Rich Lowry, "Against the Balanced-Budget Amendment," *National Review* online, July 19, 2011. www.nationalreview.com.

3. What two wars does the author refer to in support of his view that military spending can be necessary without declaration of war on nation-states?

If Congress has trouble staying within constitutional bounds now, just wait until the Constitution mandates that it must balance the federal budget.

The Call for a Balanced-Budget Amendment

Republicans have made a late entry into the debt-ceiling debate with a push for adding such a requirement to the Constitution. The balanced-budget amendment is not only an implausible way out of the debt-ceiling dilemma—it's unlikely to pass Congress with the necessary two-thirds vote to send it to the states—it risks doing the worst disservice to the Constitution since Prohibition.

The balanced-budget amendment came to prominence in the Contract With America back in the 1990s. It fell a vote short in the Senate and was soon forgotten—and deserved to be.

A simple balanced-budget amendment threatens Republican fiscal priorities; it would create even more pressure to raise taxes. A straightforward amendment recognizes no difference between balance at 24 percent of GDP [gross domestic product] and at 15 percent of GDP.

Realizing this, House Republicans have crafted a version that essentially mandates their favored fiscal policies. It requires that spending not exceed 18 percent of GDP and stipulates that only a two-thirds majority can raise taxes. Only modesty, presumably, prevented the amendment's authors from spelling out budgetary levels for the Department of Health and Human Services.

The Risk of Amending the Constitution

The Constitution is meant to set out the basic rules of the road for American governance. It's not an appropriate vehicle for en-

Debt and National Security

There's near-unanimous agreement—going all the way back through the Founding Fathers and Adam Smith—that the federal government's first and foremost responsibility is to provide national security. . . . Getting national security wrong just to get somebody's accounting number right is suicidally stupid. Getting national security right means investing for the future, and as the federal government demonstrated during the Reagan era, investing for the future frequently requires borrowing money.

Steve Conover, "The Fatal Flaws of a Balanced Budget Amendment," American, *November 8, 2011. www.american.com.*

shrining transitory or controversial policy preferences. This is what the 18th Amendment establishing Prohibition did, and so ensured widespread defiance of the nation's foundational law.

A balanced-budget amendment could befall the same fate at the hands of the fiscal bootleggers of Congress. Even House Republicans voted for a budget that doesn't balance the federal books until roughly 2030. It's easy to imagine Congress playing definitional games to evade the strictures of the amendment, inevitably inviting lawsuits.

That the amendment would precipitate legal action is acknowledged in the amendment's own language: "No court of the United States or of any State shall order any increase in revenue to enforce this article." Judicial interventions in budgetary matters are, by implication, acceptable so long as they bring spending cuts. Let's hope the federal courts are packed with judges favoring Medicare reform.

Exceptions to the Amendment

The Republican amendment acknowledges there are circumstances when the budget shouldn't necessarily be balanced. It allows for a waiver in fiscal years in which a declaration of war against a nation-state is in effect. As a plot to get Nancy Pelosi to declare war on Switzerland or another handy inoffensive country, this is brilliant. Otherwise, it's wholly inadequate.

We haven't declared war on anyone since World War II. The amendment's exception wouldn't have accounted for the Cold War or the War on Terror, neither of which entailed declarations of war on nation-states.

Another provision allows three-fifths of Congress to waive the amendment for expenditures related to a military conflict "that causes an imminent and serious threat to national security." If you believe the Cold War or the War on Terror qualifies, this could have led to constant exceptions from 1947 to 1991, and from 2001 to perhaps the present.

The impulse behind the amendment is certainly laudable—to attack the debt problem at its root. But a strictly balanced budget is not important enough to be written into the Constitution. The difference between balance and a small deficit is meaningless in the long run; it certainly doesn't rise to the level of protecting free speech or ending slavery. We ran budget deficits from 1970 to 1997, and the republic survived.

The current threat to the country is historic deficits driven by historic levels of spending. Favoring the balanced-budget amendment does nothing to address those problems in the here and now. Realistically, building the coalition necessary to pass the amendment as envisioned by Republicans would take years, by which time it will be gloriously irrelevant or altogether too late.

> *"From the standpoint of economic policy, the United States has only one party, and it is the party of profligacy."*

The United States Has a Deficit Problem That Threatens Its Future

Richard A. Posner

In the following viewpoint, Richard A. Posner argues that the growth in the US public debt is a danger to the future of the economy. Posner claims that the value of the dollar is in danger of falling, which would cause upheaval worldwide. Furthermore, he claims that the US political culture is sick and unable to make the adjustments necessary to reduce the United States' debt, while the social culture also threatens any cuts in spending. Posner is a judge for the US Seventh Circuit Court of Appeals and a senior lecturer at the University of Chicago Law School.

As you read, consider the following questions:

1. According to the author, what was the total public debt in the United States at the end of fiscal year 2009?
2. Posner says that both the Democrats and Republicans now have what similar views toward spending and taxes?

Richard A. Posner, "The Real Danger of Debt," *Foreign Policy*, February 16, 2010.

3. The author claims that what practice may be a factor in recent rises in commodity prices?

In 2000, the United States had a balanced federal budget. Today, America has a deficit problem that threatens the country's future. It is compounded by former President George W. Bush's fiscal recklessness, the economic crisis that began with September 2008's financial collapse, President Barack Obama's spending ambitions, and the mysterious ability of the weakened Republican Party to create political deadlock in Congress.

The U.S. Economy

Under Bush, spending was increased, taxes were cut, and the result was huge deficits financed by borrowing. Then came the "Great Recession," as it is being called (I call it a depression because of its probable long-term economic and political consequences). The public debt (the important component of the national debt—the part that is more than an accounting entity—that is really owed), which the Bush administration's deficits had caused to double, soared further. It soared because of falling tax revenues, rising unemployment benefits, and rising government expenditures to fight the depression (such as Obama's $787 billion stimulus plan). The public debt reached $7.5 trillion by the end of fiscal year 2009 (Sept. 30, 2009) and is expected to increase another $1.6 trillion this fiscal year [2010] and another $1.3 trillion next year. That means it may exceed $10 trillion by Sept. 30, 2011. Almost half the debt is owned by foreigners, and the interest payments to them are a drain on American wealth. Interest rates on the debt will rise as the world economy recovers, increasing competition for capital.

The United States has a deeply wounded economy. At this writing, transfer payments by the government to individuals and families (Social Security, unemployment benefits, tax credits, etc.) exceed the taxes being collected from the household sector. At the same time, private investment net of depreciation is negative. This means that private savings are being borrowed by the government, combined with the government's foreign borrowing, and then transferred to households to enable them to maintain their accustomed level of consumption. People are saving more, but government borrowing overwhelms their saving, with the result that aggregate saving—public plus private—is negative. So: negative savings, negative private investment, an incredible ratio of household debt to disposable income (1.25 to 1, though down from 1.39 to 1 in 2007), massive government borrowing to finance private consumption—not a nice combination.

When the American economy does finally recover, tax revenues will rise, unemployment benefits will fall, and depression-fighting programs will end—so annual deficits should decline. But realistically, this means only that the public debt will grow more slowly than it will be growing this year and next.

The Value of the Dollar

The international dimensions of public debt growing slowly or rapidly from a very high level deserve consideration. At some point, the value of the dollar relative to other currencies will fall; this effect will be accelerated if, as is not unlikely, the "easy money" policy of the Federal Reserve, instituted to fight the depression, results in significant inflation. A falling dollar may endanger the dollar's status as an international reserve currency. Foreign contracts are often denominated in dollars rather than in a local currency. If an oil producer in a Middle Eastern country sells oil to a refinery in a South American country, neither party may be happy to have payment made in the currency of the other party's country because by the time payment is due, the value of the currency may have changed to the advantage of the other party. By providing that payment will be made in U.S. dollars, the parties can hedge against changes in the value of the local currencies. For such hedging to be effective, however, the value of the dollar has to be stable. If it becomes unstable, the dollar may cease to be the principal international reserve currency, accounting at present for almost two-thirds of international currency reserves—a status that allows the United States to run a trade deficit (up to a point) costlessly because foreign countries need to hold U.S. dollar reserves to supply dollars in exchange for local currencies to businesses that have dollar-denominated contracts.

It is true that as growing deficits reduce the value of the dollar relative to other currencies, while making imports more expensive, American exports will grow, implying a shift of workers and capital from services to manufacturing. But the shift, reversing a long-term decline in manufacturing relative to services, maybe a painful and protracted one, just as China's transition from an export-led manufacturing economy to a domestic consumer economy is likely to be painful and protracted. Any major restructuring of a country's economy will produce heavy unemployment as a byproduct until the restructuring is complete.

The Decline of Bipartisanship

The adjustments that will be needed—if the economy does not outgrow an increasing burden of debt—to maintain the U.S. economic position in the world may be especially painful and difficult because of features of the American political scene that suggest that the country might be becoming in important respects ungovernable. The perfection of interest-group politics has brought about a situation in which, to exaggerate just a bit, taxes can't be increased, spending programs can't be cut, and new spending is irresistible. If one may judge by the Bush administration's fiscal improvidence, these tendencies are bipartisan.

America used to have a liberal and a conservative party, though both were loose coalitions lacking European-style rigid ideological uniformity. The Democrats, the liberal party, favored big government and therefore big government spending—and therefore high taxes to pay for the big spending. The conservative party, the Republicans, opposed big government and big government spending, and therefore favored low taxes. These were coherent positions. For Democrats, however, favoring heavy taxes was a political albatross, while for Republicans the albatross was opposing big government spending. Beginning with [President] Ronald Reagan and continuing with [President] George W. Bush, Republicans squared the circle by abandoning their opposition to big spending while redoubling their commitment to low taxes. Belatedly, the Obama administration has decided that while still favoring big government spending (indeed more than recent Democratic administrations have done), it too wants to keep taxes low—not as low as the Republicans want, but low enough that deficits that swamp those of the Reagan and Bush years are looming.

The decline of bipartisanship is lamentable; it is small consolation that fiscal imprudence is bipartisan. The parties play leapfrog when it comes to spending. From the standpoint of economic policy, the United States has only one party, and it is the party of profligacy.

The U.S. Social Culture

As real interest rates rise as a consequence of a growing public debt and declining demand for the U.S. dollar as an international reserve currency, U.S. savings rates will rise and, by reducing consumption expenditures, slow economic activity. Economic growth may also fall as more and more resources are poured into keeping alive elderly people, most of whom are not highly productive members of society from an economic standpoint. The United States may find itself in the same kind of downward economic spiral that developing countries often find themselves in.

American political culture is sick, but the broader social culture may also impede renewed economic progress. America's growth has been promoted by the "can-do" attitude of its people, their rejection of fatalism, their individualism—qualities conducive to innovation, ambition, and hard work. But the rejection of fatalism is also a major factor in the country's soaring medical costs, as its old people (and often their children) insist that

Forecast of Public Debt in the United States, 2011

Public Debt:	$10,458,919,452,055
Public Debt per Person:	$33,555.71
Population:	311,604,657
Total Annual Debt Increase:	16.5%

TAKEN FROM: "The Global Debt Clock," *The Economist*, accessed February 9, 2012.

every effort be made, at taxpayer expense, to extend their lives. As a result, 25 percent of Medicare costs are incurred in treating elderly people in the last few months of life. American individualism is also a barrier to fiscal belt-tightening through tax hikes or spending cuts. A can-do attitude can and often does express itself in a refusal to worry about looming crises. Americans can overcome any challenge. So not to worry! Qualities that promote a country's fortunes in one era may undermine them in another.

The Carry Trade

Because of the low U.S. inflation rate and the Federal Reserve's determination to keep interest rates very low, the dollar has become a favorite tool of the "carry trade," endangering the world economy. By borrowing U.S. dollars cheaply (because U.S. interest rates are being artificially depressed by the Federal Reserve in an effort to ease credit and by doing so stimulate economic growth) and exchanging them for foreign currencies to lend or invest, traders can earn generous profits—though not without great risk. The carry trade may be a factor in recent rises in commodity prices; indeed, there is fear of new bubbles as a result of all the dollars sloshing around in the world economy. This poses dangers for the global economy because the carry trade is susceptible to runs. If a speculator borrows dollars in the short term to minimize interest expense and uses them to buy rupees, say, and the dollar surges in value relative to the rupee, the speculator may have to sell his rupees in a hurry to repay his lenders. If so, the value of the rupee will fall farther relative to the dollar, which may precipitate a run on rupees as speculators unload them. And because of the integration of the world's financial systems, a run on a foreign currency can harm other countries' economies.

The Fed has made clear that it intends to keep short-term interest rates rock-bottom low for some time, reassuring the carry traders that the Fed is not going to pull the rug out from under them by open market operations designed to reduce U.S. bank balances, a policy that would increase the value of the dollar in relation to other currencies by reducing the amount of money in circulation (the U.S. money supply is essentially the sum of all U.S. bank balances), and by doing so would increase interest rates on dollar loans. The Obama administration is doing nothing, moreover, to prevent the dollar from falling in value relative to other currencies—the government wants it to fall in order to spur exports, import substitution, and a mild inflation—and a falling dollar makes the carry trade more profitable. The carry trader borrows dollars with which to buy currencies that can be invested at higher interest rates than the cost of borrowing the dollars—and then, after cashing out the investment, he returns to the lenders dollars worth less than when he borrowed them.

The Greek fiscal crisis has caused the value of the dollar to rise sharply against the euro, and if this new valuation of the dollar persists it will hurt U.S. exports and could also trigger a crisis in the carry trade. This is a further illustration of how globally connected the U.S. economy has become—and why getting America's fiscal house in order is an urgent priority.

Viewpoint 4

> *"Economic recovery will lower the deficit, but not enough. Additional measures will be necessary to stop debt from rising to potentially dangerous levels."*

The United States Needs to Address Two Distinct Budget Deficits

Henry J. Aaron

In the following viewpoint, Henry J. Aaron argues that the public debate about deficit spending is being sidetracked by a focus on social insurance spending, instead of addressing a near-term deficit reduction. Aaron refers to these as two deficits, believing that the plan to cut costs on social insurance is one that will not yield immediate results, whereas the need to reduce the US debt immediately necessitates a plan to cut other spending. Aaron is the Bruce and Virginia MacLaury Chair senior fellow in the Economic Studies program at the Brookings Institution.

As you read, consider the following questions:

1. Aaron identifies the near-term deficit challenge as one of preventing government debt from rising faster than what?

Henry J. Aaron, "A Tale of Two Deficits: Stop Treating Them Like They're the Same Thing!," *New Republic*, June 1, 2011.

2. According to the author, current projections show that without intervention the total debt will cross the 100 percent threshold between what years?
3. The US budget deficit equals what percent of the gross domestic product, according to Aaron?

Listening to today's debates, one might think that the United States faces *a* budget deficit. Not so. America faces *two* budget deficits. The first challenge is near term. Once the economic recovery is well-advanced, we must find a way to cut spending or raise taxes to prevent government debt from rising faster than income. The second challenge is dual: to slow the growth of health care spending, in general, and Medicare spending, in particular, and to decide whether to make cuts to Social Security. Treating the two budget challenges as one, however, just hampers efforts at finding an adequate solution to either.

Cuts to Social Insurance

To understand why the debate about the role and size of social insurance is largely independent from the debate about closing the near-term deficit, consider the proposals advanced by House Budget Committee chairman, Representative Paul Ryan. The Medicare conversion he proposes would not take effect until 2023. The plan makes no mention of Social Security. In the past, Ryan has proposed pension cuts, but only after a delay of seven years. Likewise, various budget commissions have endorsed long-term changes in Social Security. None, however, has suggested changes that would save more than a pittance over the next decade.

The bipartisan unwillingness to cut benefits for people who are retired or nearing retirement is based on two solid foundations. First, it is bad policy. People who are retired or about to retire would have no time to adjust to major cutbacks in Social Security and Medicare. Belying talk of greedy geezers, median income of people over age 65 was less than $25,000 a year in

2008. Fewer than one in four had income over $50,000. Added work may be an option for some, but not for most. Second, it is bad politics. The elderly vote in large numbers. They would, with justification, punish elected officials who renege abruptly on longstanding promises. That is why implementation of most of the cuts on Social Security benefits enacted in 1983 didn't even start until 2000 and won't be fully implemented until 2022—and then only for new retirees. These two considerations explain why Representative Ryan delayed replacing Medicare with a cash voucher for twelve years.

The Near-Term Deficit

But near-term deficit reduction cannot wait that long. No one knows just how high the outstanding U.S. debt can go before investors, private and public, at home and abroad, come to doubt the nation's capacity or willingness to service that debt. Some nations, less economically robust than the United States, have gotten into trouble when their debt was less than annual output, but the prevailing consensus is that the United States would be well advised to prevent its total debt from exceeding its annual income, particularly because so much of that debt is held abroad and the United States is currently running large trade deficits as well. Under current projections, the 100 percent threshold will be crossed sometime after 2020, but well before 2025. In short, the job of cutting the deficit must be finished in ten to twelve years.

Quite independently, a debate over the size and role of social insurance is entirely appropriate and salutary. The nation's two principal social insurance programs are too big and too central to the lives of individual Americans and to the functioning of the entire economy to escape scrutiny as circumstances change and views evolve. It is necessary, as well, for the nation to debate how best to rein in the growth of health care spending. Whether or not measures to slow the growth of spending on these two programs prove eventually to be necessary, they cannot materially affect the fiscal balance within the next decade.

The Only Solutions

Right now, however, the U.S. budget deficit equals 10 percent of gross domestic product, and one can explain the entirety of it without mentioning Medicare or Social Security. All of the current deficit and all of the deficits projected for the next decade can be explained—*fully* explained—by tax cuts enacted during the Bush administration, the costs of two wars, the economic downturn and measures to counter it, and the costs of servicing the resulting debt. Were it not for these factors, the budget today would be fully in balance.

Economic recovery will lower the deficit, but not enough. Additional measures will be necessary to stop debt from rising to potentially dangerous levels. Cuts in Medicare and Social Security spending, as a practical matter, cannot be agreed to and implemented fast enough to contribute materially to meeting *that* challenge. The only solutions are cuts in other government spending or tax increases.

Cutting the nation's deficits as soon as the recovery is well under way is therefore imperative. Deciding how much the nation can and should spend on health care and pensions will be a long and tortuous debate—as is proper. But linking the two is virtually guaranteed to delay essential near term measures that would help sustain America's hard-earned and priceless reputation as the world's safest financial center.

Viewpoint 5

> *"The economic consequences of projected debt, if realized, would be devastating."*

The Large Debt Ratio in the United States Needs to Be Reduced

Nicola Moore

In the following viewpoint, Nicola Moore argues that the United States needs to reduce its debt to prevent the debt-to-GDP (gross domestic product) ratio from approaching 100 percent. Moore claims that even after the global recession ends, the ratio is likely to increase without intervention. She concludes that the Social Security, Medicare, and Medicaid entitlement programs need to be reformed to avoid the negative economic and political consequences of a higher ratio. Moore is a senior analyst for Altria and former assistant director of economic policy studies at the Heritage Foundation.

As you read, consider the following questions:

1. Moore claims that from 2007 to 2010, anti-recessionary efforts drove up advanced economies' deficits collectively by what percent of gross domestic product?

Nicola Moore, "US Long-Term Debt Situation Is One of the World's Worst," Heritage Foundation WebMemo, no. 2972, July 27, 2010. www.heritage.org.

2. The author points to a study by the Bank for International Settlements (BIS) finding that if the United States follows the status quo, by 2040 its debt-to-GDP ratio would reach what?
3. Moore claims that according to the International Monetary Fund (IMF), by 2015 the United States will have a debt-to-GDP ratio of what?

This year [2010] the U.S. public debt is projected to reach 62 percent of the economy—up from 40 percent in 2008 and nearly double the historical average, according to recent Congressional Budget Office (CBO) estimates. The financial crisis and recession drove much of this debt swing, yet larger problems loom in the future.

Debt Around the World

By 2030, the CBO projects that debt will more than double to 146 percent of GDP [gross domestic product]. The only good news, if it can be called that, is that the U.S. is not alone. Two recent studies by the International Monetary Fund (IMF) and the Bank for International Settlements (BIS) highlight the significance of the global debt challenge and stress the need for governments to aim higher than short-term deficit reductions. For the U.S., one of the most poorly positioned countries, addressing the long-term debt challenge must include prompt reform of Social Security, Medicare, and Medicaid.

Since 2007, nations across the globe have been following a recipe for rising debt. Government financing surged to ameliorate the global financial crisis, amounting to 13.2 percent of industrialized countries' GDP. Meanwhile, a worldwide recession caused revenues to drop, growth to slow, and politicians to pursue false hopes that lavish stimulus spending would somehow stop the bleeding. These anti-recessionary efforts drove advanced economies' deficits collectively up to 20–30 percent of GDP in three years.

The numbers are alarming enough, but as the BIS points out, the most damning aspect is that these deficits are now baked into the cake—otherwise known as structural deficits—and will persist even when economies recover. A short-term focus on deficit reduction, such as G20 nations' pledges to halve deficits by 2013, will do little to pull nations back from the brink. The U.S. domestic situation is so severe that a fiscal adjustment of 12 percent of GDP would be required to stabilize debt at 60 percent of GDP, which is even higher than Greece's 9.2 percent adjustment.

Debt Projections in the Future

The main driver of medium- and long-term liabilities is that governments are on the hook for trillions in unfunded age-related spending for pension and health care obligations. Over the next 20 years, the U.S. will experience the second highest projected increase of all the G20 countries in health care and pension spending as a share of GDP.

To assess the impact of age-related spending, the BIS ran three spending scenarios to project debt through 2040 in 12 countries. In all scenarios debt was found to reach unsustainable levels.

The first scenario followed the status quo in which countries' public debt ranged from 250 percent to 600 percent of GDP. The second scenario introduced gradual adjustments that would halve deficits in the short term, yet debt still reached levels ranging from 100 percent to 400 percent. The third scenario added an age-related spending freeze (at 2011 levels) to scenario two, and only four countries (Italy, Germany, Austria, and the Netherlands) lowered debt levels below 100 percent of GDP.

The U.S. was one of the worst performers, reaching debt levels in each scenario of 450, 300, and 200 percent of GDP, respectively. That debt is primarily driven by the unfunded obligations held by Social Security, Medicare, and Medicaid.

The Importance of the Debt Ratio

The heavy coverage of annual budget deficit dollar figures vastly outweighs their economic importance. To the extent that government debt is significant, cumulative publicly held debt as a percentage of the nation's income is the more relevant figure. After all, the total debt owed is much more significant than how much that debt increased over the past 12 months (which is what the deficit measures). Whether that debt level is manageable depends on total income; Bill Gates, for instance, could afford a much higher debt load than the typical American family. Hence, banks use the "debt ratio"—total debt as a percentage of income—to determine the level at which borrowing families and businesses can afford to owe.

Brian M. Riedl, "Ten Myths About Budget Deficits and Debt," Backgrounder, *no. 2178, September 8, 2008.*

After the Global Recession

One of the largest challenges BIS predicts nations will face is that economic output is unlikely to fully recover after the global recession ends. Deficits will likely persist, causing the debt-to-GDP ratio to rise steadily. This would result in serious economic pains.

First, upward pressure will be put on interest rates. As sovereign debt rises, more resources will be required to purchase it, and the risks associated with potential loss will rise. As a result, debt buyers will require better interest premiums. In an earlier study, the IMF has estimated that a 10 percentage point increase in the debt ratio would cause interest rates to rise by approximately 50 basis points. For the U.S., interest rates could climb by 2 full percentage points, which would cause the cost of debt to explode over the long term.

Second, as more economic resources are required to service a country's debt, fewer resources are available for the private sector to invest in productive capital. For countries like the U.S. that borrow excessively from abroad, this problem will be exacerbated because debt service payments will be paid outside the U.S. economy. The IMF estimates that a debt increase of 10 percentage points depresses investment as a percentage of GDP by roughly 0.4 points.

Third, the drop off in investment slows economic growth. An increase in the debt-to-GDP ratio of 10 percentage points would slow growth by 0.15 to 0.2 percentage points per year, according to the IMF. While that number may seem slight, compounded over several years, the impact becomes severe.

Finally, significant inflationary pressure will result from high levels of debt. On one hand, if debt buyers lose their appetite for buying debt, then monetary authorities would have to print money to continue to fund the debt. On the other hand, inflation could be used to erode the value of existing debt by lowering the real value of currency and, thus, the real value of the stock of debt. Indeed, inflation was partly responsible for enabling the U.S. to bring down its debt so rapidly after World War I. Either way, the result is bad for consumers and savers, who see their purchasing power and savings drop.

Concern About Debt Levels

With such significant consequences at stake, it is no wonder that the IMF monitors government debt levels very carefully. By 2015, advanced economies are projected to carry an average debt of 110 percent of GDP, with the U.S. trailing at 83 percent. While that is not as bad as Greece, for instance, debt that approaches 100 percent of GDP can trigger an IMF audit. This would be a fiscal embarrassment that would erode U.S. global economic leadership.

The BIS stresses that "consolidations along the lines currently being discussed [by global leaders] will not be sufficient to ensure that debt levels remain within reasonable bounds over the next several decades."

Most strikingly, it also notes that tax increases would most likely not close the gap, either: "Given the level of taxes in some countries, one has to wonder if further increases will actually raise revenue."

The Need for Reform

For the U.S., legislative and policy reforms to Social Security, Medicare, and Medicaid should include the following:

- *Report long-term obligations.* Congress fails to report the unfunded obligations of entitlements in its annual budget. This number should be prominently disclosed in the budget, and Congress should be required to have a stand-alone vote on any policy that would substantially add to that number.
- *Create long-term budgets for entitlements.* Entitlements grow on autopilot, without annual review, and have first call on federal dollars. Instead, entitlements should be placed on limited, 30-year budgets that would be reviewed and debated by Congress every five years. This would put entitlement spending on a level playing field with other priorities and force Congress to spend within its means.
- *Make retirement programs fair but affordable.* Entitlement spending promises debt-financed benefits for all retirees, regardless of income. Meanwhile, a welcome increase in life expectancy has resulted in unwelcome years of unaffordable benefits. To resolve these issues, entitlements should be better targeted to those most in need, and the eligibility age for these programs should be increased with longevity.

The warning shots fired by the IMF and BIS should be a wake-up call to global leaders to get public debt under control. The economic consequences of projected debt, if realized, would be devastating, and the prospect of triggering an IMF audit is embarrassing at best and politically untenable at worst.

In the U.S., the best way to prevent this disaster is to start with serious and prompt reform to age-related spending in Social Security, Medicare, and Medicaid entitlements.

> *"We should worry less about debt ratios and thresholds, and more about our inability to see these indicators for the artificial—and often irrelevant—constructs that they are."*

A Large Debt Ratio Is Not Necessarily a Problem

Robert J. Shiller

In the following viewpoint, Robert J. Shiller argues that although some people believe the ratio between public debt and gross domestic product (GDP) is significant, it is in fact an arbitrary measure. Shiller contends that there is no evidence that a high debt-to-GDP ratio causes economic trouble and, in fact, the causality may go the other way. Shiller is the Arthur M. Okun Professor of Economics at Yale University. He is the author of The Subprime Solution: How Today's Global Financial Crisis Happened, and What to Do about It.

As you read, consider the following questions:

1. The author claims that people think a country becomes insolvent when its debt exceeds what percent of its gross domestic product (GDP)?

Robert J. Shiller, "Debt and Delusion," *Project Syndicate*, July 21, 2011. www.project-syndicate.org.

2. Shiller contends that what is really causing Greece's economic crisis is not its debt-to-GDP ratio, but what?
3. According to the author, if economic trouble causes the debt-to-GDP ratio to rise, then do countries need to avoid a high ratio?

Economists like to talk about thresholds that, if crossed, spell trouble. Usually there is an element of truth in what they say. But the public often overreacts to such talk.

Debt and GDP

Consider, for example, the debt-to-GDP [gross domestic product] ratio, much in the news nowadays in Europe and the United States. It is sometimes said, almost in the same breath, that Greece's debt equals 153% of its annual GDP, and that Greece is insolvent. Couple these statements with recent television footage of Greeks rioting in the street. Now, what does that look like?

Here in the US, it might seem like an image of our future, as public debt comes perilously close to 100% of annual GDP and continues to rise. But maybe this image is just a bit too vivid in our imaginations. Could it be that people think that a country becomes insolvent when its debt exceeds 100% of GDP?

That would clearly be nonsense. After all, debt (which is measured in currency units) and GDP (which is measured in currency units per unit of time) yields a ratio in units of pure time. There is nothing special about using a year as that unit. A year is the time that it takes for the earth to orbit the sun, which, except for seasonal industries like agriculture, has no particular economic significance.

We should remember this from high school science: always pay attention to units of measurement. Get the units wrong and you are totally befuddled.

If economists did not habitually annualize quarterly GDP data and multiply quarterly GDP by four, Greece's debt-to-GDP ratio would be four times higher than it is now. And if they habitually decadalized [i.e. used total GDP over 10 years as the standard measure] GDP, multiplying the quarterly GDP numbers by 40 instead of four, Greece's debt burden would be 15%. From the standpoint of Greece's ability to pay, such units would be more relevant, since it doesn't have to pay off its debts fully in one year (unless the crisis makes it impossible to refinance current debt).

Some of Greece's national debt is owed to Greeks, by the way. As such, the debt burden woefully understates the obligations that Greeks have to each other (largely in the form of family obligations). At any time in history, the debt-to-annual-GDP ratio (including informal debts) would vastly exceed 100%.

A Social-Feedback Mechanism

Most people never think about this when they react to the headline debt-to-GDP figure. Can they really be so stupid as to get mixed up by these ratios? Speaking from personal experience, I have to say that they can, because even I, a professional economist, have occasionally had to stop myself from making exactly the same error.

Economists who adhere to rational-expectations models of the world will never admit it, but a lot of what happens in markets is driven by pure stupidity—or, rather, inattention, misinformation about fundamentals, and an exaggerated focus on currently circulating stories.

What is really happening in Greece is the operation of a social-feedback mechanism. Something started to cause investors to fear that Greek debt had a slightly higher risk of eventual default. Lower demand for Greek debt caused its price to fall, meaning that its yield in terms of market interest rates rose. The higher rates made it more costly for Greece to refinance its debt, creating a fiscal crisis that has forced the government to impose severe austerity measures, leading to public unrest and an economic collapse that has fueled even greater investor skepticism about Greece's ability to service its debt.

This feedback has nothing to do with the debt-to-annual-GDP ratio crossing some threshold, unless the people who contribute to the feedback believe in the ratio. To be sure, the ratio is a factor that would help us to assess risks of negative feedback, since the government must refinance short-term debt sooner, and, if the crisis pushes up interest rates, the authorities will face intense pressures for fiscal austerity sooner or later. But the ratio is not the cause of the feedback.

An Inconclusive Study

A paper written last year by Carmen Reinhart and Kenneth Rogoff, called "Growth in a Time of Debt," has been widely quoted for its analysis of 44 countries over 200 years, which found that when government debt exceeds 90% of GDP, countries suffer slower growth, losing about one percentage point on the annual rate.

One might be misled into thinking that, because 90% sounds awfully close to 100%, awful things start happening to countries that get into such a mess. But if one reads their paper carefully, it is clear that Reinhart and Rogoff picked the 90% figure almost arbitrarily. They chose, without explanation, to divide debt-to-GDP ratios into the following categories: under 30%, 30–60%, 60–90%, and over 90%. And it turns out that growth rates decline in *all* of these categories as the debt-to-GDP ratio increases, only somewhat more in the last category.

There is also the issue of reverse causality. Debt-to-GDP ratios tend to increase for countries that are in economic trouble. If this is part of the reason that higher debt-to-GDP ratios correspond to lower economic growth, there is less reason to think that countries should avoid a higher ratio, as Keynesian theory implies that fiscal austerity would undermine, rather than boost, economic performance.

The fundamental problem that much of the world faces today is that investors are overreacting to debt-to-GDP ratios, fearful of some magic threshold, and demanding fiscal-austerity programs too soon. They are asking governments to cut expenditure while their economies are still vulnerable. Households are running scared, so they cut expenditures as well, and businesses are being dissuaded from borrowing to finance capital expenditures.

The lesson is simple: We should worry less about debt ratios and thresholds, and more about our inability to see these indicators for the artificial—and often irrelevant—constructs that they are.

Periodical and Internet Sources Bibliography

The following articles have been selected to supplement the diverse views presented in this chapter.

Henry J. Aaron	"The Central Question for Health Policy in Deficit Reduction," *New England Journal of Medicine*, October 12, 2011.
Steve Chapman	"The Balanced-Budget Amendment Delusion," Reason .com, November 28, 2011.
William A. Galston	"America Will Fix Its Debt Problem, Once It's Exhausted the Alternatives," *Financial Times*, July 14, 2011.
Doug Kendall and Dahlia Lithwick	"Off Balance: The Balanced Budget Amendment Would Make the Framers Weep," *Slate*, July 15, 2011. www.slate.com.
Annie Lowrey	"Abolish the Debt Ceiling! It's a Pointless, Dangerous Historical Relic," *Slate*, May 16, 2011. www .slate.com.
John H. Makin	"Getting to Deficit Reduction," *Economic Outlook*, March 2011. www.aei.org.
Norman J. Ornstein	"Why a Balanced-Budget Amendment Is Too Risky," *Washington Post*, July 18, 2011.
Richard W. Rahn	"Time for a Constitutional Fix," *Washington Times*, August 16, 2011.
Michael D. Tanner	"Beware the Balanced Approach," *National Interest*, November 16, 2011.
George Zornick	"The Paradoxical, Dangerous Balanced Budget Amendment," *Nation*, July 6, 2011. www.the nation.com.

Chapter 3

How Do Government Spending Policies Affect the Economy?

Chapter Preface

In February 2009, the US Congress passed The American Recovery and Reinvestment Act of 2009, also known as the Recovery Act, in response to the economic recession. The Recovery Act has three goals: to create new jobs and protect existing jobs; to spur economic activity and invest in economic growth; and to promote accountability and transparency in government spending. The Recovery Act planned for $787 billion to be spent in three areas: tax cuts and benefits for families and businesses; funding for federal contracts, grants, and loans; and funding for entitlement programs. In 2011, the original spending estimate was increased to $840 billion. Three years after its enactment, with $749 billion already paid out, there is wide disagreement about whether or not the Recovery Act has helped the economy.

According to the US government, in the first three years of the Recovery Act almost three-quarters of a trillion dollars was spent. Approximately $300 billion was spent through tax benefits. The bulk of that amount—approximately $250 billion—came in the form of tax credits for individuals and families, such as the First-Time Homebuyer tax credit, the Earned Income tax credit, and the Making Work Pay tax credit. More than $33 billion went to tax incentives for businesses, such as the Work Opportunity tax credit. More than $10 billion went to individuals and businesses in tax credits for making energy efficient improvements.

During the Recovery Act's first three years, more than $225 billion was spent on federal contracts, grants, and loans. The bulk of this spending—almost $90 billion—went toward education. This includes spending given to the states to prevent layoffs and cutbacks in public schools and increases in financial aid for college students. More than $33 billion went to funding for transportation, including improvements to roads, railroads, and airports. More than $26 billion went to infrastructure, which includes broadband development and funds for federal buildings. Almost $24 billion went for programs meant to increase energy efficiency and clean up the environment. Housing programs, research programs, and health programs also received more than $10 billion each in federal contracts, grants, and loans.

Another area of spending under the Recovery Act was entitlement programs, with more than $222 billion spent in the first three years. Almost $90 billion went to help meet gaps in funding for Medicaid and Medicare, programs that offer health coverage to low-income and disabled people. More than $60 billion went toward funding unemployment insurance, including several extensions of benefits passed by Congress due to continued high unemployment. Almost $40 billion went toward family services, including assistance to needy families and food stamps.

Opinions differ on whether the spending under the Recovery Act created jobs, saved jobs, and spurred economic activity. Some critics, such as economist Kevin A. Hassett, argue that the stimulus spending has not worked: "Given this lengthy period of slow growth, it was a mistake for the Obama administration to pursue short-term Keynesian stimulus." Others, such as economist Paul Krugman have the opposite view: "America needed a much stronger program than what it actually got . . . the inadequacy of the stimulus was obvious from the beginning." Thus, even if the Recovery Act did not completely revive the economy, it is clear that this will not resolve the conflict between those who believe stimulus spending helps the economy and those who believe it does not. The viewpoints in this chapter illustrate the deep division in perspectives on the economic wisdom of stimulus spending.

VIEWPOINT 1

> *"The central objective of national economic policy until sustained recovery is firmly established must be increasing confidence, borrowing and lending, and spending."*

Increased Stimulus Spending Can Help End the Recession

Lawrence H. Summers

In the following viewpoint, Lawrence H. Summers argues that for a successful economic recovery, the US government must pursue measures that increase confidence, borrowing, and spending. Summers contends that the reason the recession continues is due to lack of demand; although too much spending was part of what caused the crisis, an increase in spending to increase demand is the cure. Summers is the Charles W. Eliot University Professor at Harvard University's Kennedy School of Government and former director of the National Economic Council under President Barack Obama.

As you read, consider the following questions:

1. According to Summers, by how many percentage points has the amount of the population working fallen from 2006 to 2011?

Lawrence H. Summers, "More Stimulus Needed for Jobs Crisis," Reuters, June 13, 2011.

2. The author claims that within a couple of years of the two deep recessions after World War II, the US economy was growing by at least how much a year?
3. Summers suggests spending measures that he claims will have a near term cost of how much?

Even with the massive 2008–2009 policy effort that successfully prevented financial collapse and Depression, the United States is now half way to a lost economic decade. Over the last 5 years, from the first quarter of 2006 to the first quarter of 2011, the U.S. economy's growth rate averaged less than 1 percent a year, about like Japan during the period when its bubble burst. At the same time the fraction of the population working has fallen from 63.1 to 58.4 percent, reducing the number of those with jobs by more than 10 million. The fraction of the population working remains almost exactly at its recession trough and recent reports suggest that growth is slowing.

A Lack of Demand

Beyond the lack of jobs and incomes, an economy producing below its potential for a prolonged interval sacrifices its future. To an extent that once would have been unimaginable, new college graduates are this month moving back in with their parents because they have no job or means of support. Strapped school districts across the country are cutting out advanced courses in math and science and in some cases only opening school 4 days a week. And reduced incomes and tax collections at present and in the future are the most important cause of unacceptable budget deficits at present and in the future.

You cannot prescribe for a malady unless you diagnose it accurately and understand its causes. Recessions are times when there is too little demand for the products of businesses, and so they fail to employ all those who want to work. That the problem in a period of high unemployment like the present one is a lack of business demand for employees, not any lack of desire to work is all but self-evident. It is demonstrated by the observations that (i) the propensity of workers to quit jobs and the level of job openings are at near-record low levels; (ii) rises in nonemployment have taken place among essentially all demographic skill and education groups; and (iii) rising rates of profit and falling rates of wage growth suggest that it is employers, not workers, who have the power in almost every market.

I belabor the idea that lack of demand is the fundamental cause of economies producing below their potential because the failure to recognize the centrality of demand can have catastrophic consequences. But for [German leader Adolf] Hitler and the military buildup up he caused, FDR [US president Franklin D. Roosevelt] would have left office in early 1941 a failure, with American unemployment above 15 percent and with the recovery promise of the New Deal shattered by the premature attempt in 1937 to reassert the traditional virtues of deficit reduction and inflation control. When I entered the Clinton administration in 1993, it was generally believed that Japan had the potential to grow its economy by 4 percent a year going forward, enough to have doubled output from that time until now. Instead output has barely grown, a consequence of the post-bubble stagnation that Japan suffered.

A sick economy constrained by demand works very differently than a normal one. Measures that usually promote growth and job creation can have little effect or can actually backfire. When demand is constraining an economy, there is little to be gained from increasing potential supply. In a recession, if more people seek to borrow less or save more, there is reduced demand and hence fewer jobs. Training programs or measures to increase work incentives for those with both high and low incomes may affect who gets the jobs, but in a demand-constrained economy will not affect the total number of jobs. Most paradoxically, measures that increase productivity and efficiency, if they do not also translate into increased demand, may actually reduce the number of people working as the level of total output remains demand constrained.

Recovery from Recession

Traditionally, the American economy has recovered robustly from recession as demand has been quickly renewed. Within a couple of years after the only two deep recessions of the post World War II period—those of 1974–1975 and 1980–1982—the economy was growing in the range of 6 percent or more—rates that seem inconceivable today. Why?

Inflation dynamics defined the traditional post-War American business cycle. Recoveries continued and sometimes even accelerated until they were murdered by the Federal Reserve with inflation control as the motive. When the Fed became concerned about inflation accelerating, usually too late, it raised interest rates and crunched credit, stifling housing, business investment, and consumer durable purchases and causing the economy to go into recession. After inflation slowed, rapid recovery propelled by dramatic reductions in interest rates and a backlog of deferred investment was almost inevitable.

Our current situation is very different. With more prudent monetary policies, expansions are no longer cut short by rising inflation and the Fed hitting the brakes. All three American expansions since [Chairman of the Federal Reserve] Paul Volcker brought inflation back under control have run long. They end after a period of overconfidence drives the prices of capital assets too high and the apparent increases in wealth give rise to excessive borrowing, lending and spending.

After bubbles burst there is no pent up desire to invest. Instead there is a glut of capital caused by overinvestment during the period of confidence—vacant houses, malls without tenants, and factories without customers. At the same time, consumers discover that they have less wealth than they expected, less collateral to borrow against and are under more pressure than they expected from their creditors. Little wonder that private spending collapses and that post bubble economic downturns often last more than a decade and are only ended through external events like military buildups.

Pressure on private spending is enhanced by structural changes. Take as a vivid example the publishing industry. As local bookstores have given way to megastores, megastores have given way to internet retailers, and internet retailers have given way to ebooks, two things have happened. The economy's productive potential has increased and its ability to generate demand that fulfills the potential has been compromised as resources have been transferred from middle class retail and wholesale workers with a high propensity to spend up the scale to those with a much lower propensity to spend. And the need for capital investment in distribution networks has come down.

The Solution

What then is to be done? This is no time for fatalism or traditional political agendas that the two parties have pushed in more normal times. The central irony of financial crisis is that while it is caused by too much confidence, borrowing and lending, and spending, it is only resolved by increases in confidence, borrowing and lending, and spending. It follows that the central objective of national economic policy until sustained recovery is firmly established must be increasing confidence, borrowing and lending, and spending. Unless and until this is done, other policies, no matter how apparently appealing or effective in normal times, will be futile at best.

We should recognize that it is a false economy to defer infrastructure maintenance and replacement and instead take advantage of the a moment when 10-year interest rates are below 3 percent and construction unemployment approaches 20 percent to expand infrastructure investment.

It is far too soon for financial policy to shift towards preventing future bubbles and possible inflation and away from assuring adequate demand. The underlying rate of inflation is still trending downward and the problems of insufficient borrowing and investing exceed any problems of overconfidence. The Dodd-Frank [Wall Street Reform and Consumer Protection

Act] legislation is a broadly appropriate response to the hugely important challenge of preventing any recurrence of the events of 2008. It needs to be vigorously implemented. But under-, not over-confidence is the problem of the moment and needs to be the focus of policy.

The Danger of Slow Growth

More concretely, the fiscal debate needs to take on board the reality that the greatest threat to the nation's creditworthiness is a sustained period of slow growth that, as in southern Europe, causes debt-GDP [gross domestic product] ratios to soar. This means that essential discussions about medium-term measures to restrain spending and raise revenues need to be coupled with a focus on near-term growth. Without the payroll tax cuts and unemployment insurance negotiated by the President and Congress last fall [2010] we might well be looking today at the possibility of a double dip. Substantial withdrawal of fiscal support for demand at the end of 2011 would be premature. Fiscal support should be continued and indeed expanded by providing the payroll tax cut to employers as well as employees. Raising the share of the payroll tax cut from 2% to 3% would be desirable as well. At a near term cost of a little over $200 billion, these measures offer the prospect of significant improvement in economic performance over the next few years translating into significant increases in the tax base and reductions in necessary government outlays.

It is appropriate that policy in other dimensions be informed by the shortage of demand that is a defining characteristic of our economy. For example, the Obama administration is doing important work in promoting export growth by modernizing export controls, promoting U.S. products abroad and reaching and enforcing trade agreements. Much more could be done through changes in visa policy, for example, to promote exports of tourism as well as education and health services. In a similar vein recent Presidential directives regarding relaxation of inappropriate regulatory burdens should be rigorously implemented to boost confidence.

All of this is important, even essential. But the place to start is with the Hippocratic Oath—Do No Harm. And that means that every measure that comes out of Washington needs to be evaluated on the basis that it will not reduce the demand for goods and services at a time when America's economy has been and will remain profoundly demand constrained.

> *"Repeated failed attempts in America and abroad have shown that governments cannot spend their way out of recessions."*

Increased Stimulus Spending Will Not End the Recession

Brian Riedl

In the following viewpoint, Brian Riedl argues that government spending does not stimulate economic growth. Riedl contends that several attempts to end recessions through stimulus spending have failed. He claims that government spending merely moves money that would have been spent elsewhere, frequently in an inefficient manner, increasing future debt while failing to create jobs. Riedl is the former Graver M. Hermann Fellow in Federal Budgetary Affairs in the Thomas A. Roe Institute for Economic Policy Studies at The Heritage Foundation.

As you read, consider the following questions:

1. According to the author, how many net jobs were lost in 2009?

Brian Riedl, "Why Government Spending Does Not Stimulate Economic Growth: Answering the Critics," Heritage Foundation *Backgrounder*, no. 2354, pp. 1–5, 9. January 5, 2010. www.heritage.org.

2. Riedl claims that according to the Keynesian stimulus theory models, $1.4 trillion in deficit spending should have created new economic activity worth what?
3. According to Riedl, large stimulus bills often reduce long-term productivity by transferring resources from what sector to the government?

Proponents of President Barack Obama's $787 billion stimulus bill continue to insist that the massive government bailout played a decisive role in moving the economy out of the recession. Yet assuming no destructive government actions, the economy's self-correction mechanism was widely expected to move the economy out of recession in 2009 anyway. With a parade of "stimulus" bills the past two years (going back to President George W. Bush's tax rebate in early 2008), it was entirely predictable that some would link the expected end of the recession to whichever stimulus bill happened to come last.

Government Stimulus Failures

Indeed, President Obama's stimulus bill failed by its own standards. In a January 2009 report, White House economists predicted that the stimulus bill would create (not merely save) 3.3 million net jobs by 2010. Since then, 3.5 million more net jobs have been lost, pushing the unemployment rate above 10 percent. The fact that government failed to spend its way to prosperity is not an isolated incident:

- During the 1930s, New Deal lawmakers doubled federal spending—yet unemployment remained above 20 percent until World War II.
- Japan responded to a 1990 recession by passing 10 stimulus spending bills over 8 years (building the largest national debt in the industrialized world)—yet its economy remained stagnant.
- In 2001, President Bush responded to a recession by "in-

jecting" tax rebates into the economy. The economy did not respond until two years later, when tax rate reductions were implemented.

- In 2008, President Bush tried to head off the current recession with another round of tax rebates. The recession continued to worsen.
- Now, the most recent $787 billion stimulus bill was intended to keep the unemployment rate from exceeding 8 percent. In November, it topped 10 percent.

Undeterred by these repeated stimulus failures, President Obama is calling for yet another stimulus bill. There is every reason to expect another round to fail as miserably as the past ones, and it would bury the nation deeper in debt.

The Stimulus Myth

The economic theory behind the stimulus builds on the work of John Maynard Keynes eight decades ago. It begins with the idea that an economic shock has left demand persistently and significantly below potential supply. As people stop spending money, businesses pull back production, and the ensuing vicious circle of falling demand and production shrinks the economy.

Keynesians believe that government spending can make up this shortfall in private demand. Their models assume that—in an underperforming economy—government spending adds money to the economy, taxes remove money from the economy, and so the increase in the budget deficit represents net new dollars injected. Therefore, it scarcely matters how the dollars are spent. Keynes is said to have famously asserted that a government program that pays people to dig and refill ditches would provide new income for those workers to spend and circulate through the economy, creating even more jobs and income.

The Keynesian argument also assumes that consumption spending adds to immediate economic growth while savings do not. By this reasoning, unemployment benefits, food stamps, and low-income tax rebates are among the most effective stimulus policies because of their likelihood to be consumed rather than saved.

Taking this analysis to its logical extreme, Mark Zandi of Economy.com has boiled down the government's influence on America's broad and diverse $14 trillion economy into a simple menu of stimulus policy options, whereby Congress can decide how much economic growth it wants and then pull the appropriate levers. Zandi asserts that for each dollar of new government spending: temporary food stamps adds $1.73 to the economy, extended unemployment benefits adds $1.63, increased infrastructure spending adds $1.59, and aid to state and local governments adds $1.38. Jointly, these figures imply that, in a recession, a typical dollar in new deficit spending expands the economy by roughly $1.50. Over the past 40 years, this idea of government spending as stimulus has fallen out of favor among many economists. As this paper shows, it is contradicted both by empirical data and economic logic.

The Evidence Is In

Economic data contradict Keynesian stimulus theory. If deficits represented "new dollars" in the economy, the record $1.2 trillion in FY [fiscal year] 2009 deficit spending that began in October 2008—well before the stimulus added $200 billion more—would have already overheated the economy. Yet despite the historic 7 percent increase in GDP [gross domestic product] deficit spending over the previous year, the economy shrank by 2.3 percent in FY 2009. To argue that deficits represent new money injected into the economy is to argue that the economy would have contracted by 9.3 percent without this "infusion" of added deficit spending (or even more, given the Keynesian multiplier effect that was supposed to further boost the impact). That is simply not plausible, and few if any economists have claimed otherwise.

And if the original $1.2 trillion in deficit spending failed to slow the economy's slide, there was no reason to believe that adding $200 billion more in 2009 deficit spending from the stimu-

The Keynesian Stimulus Theory

The Keynesian stimulus theory fails for the simple reason that it is only half a theory. It correctly describes how deficit spending can raise the level of demand in part of the economy, and ignores how government borrowing to finance deficit spending automatically reduces demand elsewhere. Exculpatory allusions to idle saving simply do not wash in a modern economy supported by a modern financial system. Deficit spending does not create real purchasing power and so it cannot increase total demand in the economy. Deficit spending can only shift the pattern of demand toward government-centric preferences.

Empirical research rarely provides a simple, single answer to a policy question, and examinations of Keynesian stimulus are no exception. Yet the available results consistently indicate that, using a modern macroeconomic model and treating monetary policy carefully, Keynesian stimulus's short-term effects lie somewhere in the narrow range between slim and none. Keynesian stimulus produces debt, not jobs.

J.D. Foster, "Keynesian Fiscal Stimulus Policies Stimulate Debt—Not the Economy," Backgrounder, *no. 2302, July 27, 2009. www.heritage.org.*

lus bill would suddenly do the trick. Proponents of yet another stimulus should answer the following questions: (1) If nearly $1.4 trillion budget deficits are not enough stimulus, how much is enough? (2) If Keynesian stimulus repeatedly fails, why still rely on the theory?

This is no longer a theoretical exercise. The idea that increased deficit spending can cure recessions has been tested repeatedly, and it has failed repeatedly. The economic models that assert that every $1 of deficit spending grows the economy by $1.50 cannot explain why $1.4 trillion in deficit spending did not create a $2.1 trillion explosion of new economic activity.

Why Government Spending Fails

Moving forward, the important question is *why* government spending fails to end recessions. Spending-stimulus advocates claim that Congress can "inject" new money into the economy, increasing demand and therefore production. This raises the obvious question: From where does the government acquire the money it pumps into the economy? Congress does not have a vault of money waiting to be distributed. Every dollar Congress injects *into* the economy must first be taxed or borrowed *out of* the economy. No new spending power is created. It is merely redistributed from one group of people to another.

Congress cannot create new purchasing power out of thin air. If it funds new spending with taxes, it is simply redistributing existing purchasing power (while decreasing incentives to produce income and output). If Congress instead borrows the money from domestic investors, those investors will have that much less to invest or to spend in the private economy. If they borrow the money from foreigners, the balance of payments will adjust by equally raising net imports, leaving total demand and output unchanged. Every dollar Congress spends must first come from somewhere else.

For example, many lawmakers claim that every $1 billion in highway stimulus can create 47,576 new construction jobs. But Congress must first borrow that $1 billion from the private economy, which will then *lose at least as many jobs*. Highway spending simply transfers jobs and income from one part of the economy to another. As Heritage Foundation economist Ronald Utt has explained, "The only way that $1 billion of new highway spending can create 47,576 new jobs is if the $1 billion appears out of nowhere as if it were manna from heaven." This statement has been confirmed by the Department of Transportation and the General Accounting Office (since renamed the Government Accountability Office), yet lawmakers continue to base policy on this economic fallacy.

Removing water from one end of a swimming pool and pouring it in the other end will not raise the overall water level. Similarly, taking dollars from one part of the economy and distributing it to another part of the economy will not expand the economy.

Government Spending and Economic Growth

University of Chicago economist John Cochrane adds that:

> First, if money is not going to be printed, it has to come from somewhere. If the government borrows a dollar from you, that is a dollar that you do not spend, or that you do not lend to a company to spend on new investment. Every dollar of increased government spending must correspond to one less dollar of private spending. Jobs created by stimulus spending are offset by jobs lost from the decline in private spending. We can build roads instead of factories, but fiscal stimulus can't help us to build more of both. This form of "crowding out" is just accounting, and doesn't rest on any perceptions or behavioral assumptions.
>
> Second, investment is "spending" every bit as much as is consumption. Keynesian fiscal stimulus advocates want money spent on consumption, not saved. They evaluate past stimulus programs by whether people who got stimulus money spent it on consumption goods rather than saved it. But the economy overall does not care if you buy a car, or if you lend money to a company that buys a forklift.

Government spending can affect long-term economic growth, both up and down. Economic growth is based on the growth of labor productivity and labor supply, which can be affected by how governments directly and indirectly influence the use of an economy's resources. However, increasing the economy's productivity rate—which often requires the application of new technology and resources—can take many years or even decades to materialize. It is not short-term stimulus.

In fact, large stimulus bills often reduce long-term productivity by transferring resources from the more productive private sector to the less productive government. The government rarely receives good value for the dollars it spends. However, stimulus bills provide politicians with the political justification to grant tax dollars to favored constituencies. By increasing the budget deficit, large stimulus bills eventually contribute to higher interest rates while dropping even more debt on future generations. . . .

A Failed Stimulus

All recessions eventually end. The U.S. economy has proved resilient enough to eventually overcome even the most misguided economic policies of the past. Yet it would be fallacious to credit the stimulus bill for any economic recovery that inevitably occurs in the future. According to Keynesian theory, a $1.4 trillion budget deficit should have immediately overheated the economy. According to the White House, the stimulus should have created 3.3 million net jobs. Instead, the economy remained in recession and 3.5 million more net jobs were lost. By every reasonable standard, the stimulus failed.

[American writer and literary critic] H.L. Mencken once wrote that "complex problems have simple, easy to understand, wrong answers." He may as well have been referring to the idea that Congress can foster economic growth simply by "injecting" money into the economy. Government stimulus spending is not a magic wand that creates jobs and income. Repeated failed attempts in America and abroad have shown that governments cannot spend their way out of recessions. Focusing on productivity growth builds a stronger economy over the long term—and leaves America better prepared to handle future economic downturns.

> *"As long as one political party clings to the idea that government spending kills jobs, it's hard to see how we extricate ourselves from this mess."*

Government Spending Does Not Kill Jobs

Alan S. Blinder

In the following viewpoint, Alan S. Blinder argues that government spending does not kill jobs. Disputing the opposing arguments, Blinder claims it is false that the 2009 fiscal stimulus created no jobs, there is no legitimate concern about rising interest rates, and large deficits have not slowed business investment. Furthermore, Blinder contends that it is a false dilemma that the United States must choose between more jobs or a lower deficit. Blinder is the Gordon S. Rentschler Memorial Professor of Economics and Public Affairs at Princeton University and former vice chairman of the Federal Reserve.

As you read, consider the following questions:

1. The author claims that by the reasoning that government spending kills jobs, massive cuts in public spending should cause what?
2. According to Blinder, government spending under the

Alan S. Blinder, "The GOP Myth of 'Job-Killing' Spending," *Wall Street Journal*, June 21, 2011.

Recovery Act exceeded how many billion dollars?
3. What is the author's preferred fiscal stimulus program for maximum job creation?

It was the British economist John Maynard Keynes who famously wrote that ideas, "both when they are right and when they are wrong, are more powerful than is commonly understood. Indeed, the world is ruled by little else." Right now, I'm worried about the damage that might be done by one particularly wrong-headed idea: the notion that, in stark contrast to Keynes's teaching, government spending destroys jobs.

The Argument Against Government Spending

No, that's not a typo. House speaker John Boehner and other Republicans regularly rail against "job-killing government spending." Think about that for a minute. The claim is that employment actually declines when federal spending rises. Using the same illogic, employment should soar if we made massive cuts in public spending—as some are advocating right now.

Acting on such a belief would imperil a still-shaky economy that is not generating nearly enough jobs. So let's ask: How, exactly, could more government spending "kill jobs"?

It is easy, but irrelevant, to understand how someone might object to any particular item in the federal budget—whether it is the war in Afghanistan, ethanol subsidies, Social Security benefits, or building bridges to nowhere. But even building bridges to nowhere would create jobs, not destroy them, as the congressman from nowhere knows. To be sure, that is not a valid argument for building them. Dumb public spending deserves to be rejected—but not because it kills jobs.

The Worry About Taxes

The generic conservative view that government is "too big" in some abstract sense leads to a strong predisposition against spending. OK. But the question remains: How can the government destroy jobs by either hiring people directly or buying things from private companies? For example, how is it that public purchases of computers destroy jobs but private purchases of computers create them?

One possible answer is that the taxes necessary to pay for the government spending destroy more jobs than the spending creates. That's a logical possibility, although it would require extremely inept choices of how to spend the money and how to raise the revenue. But tax-financed spending is not what's at issue today. The current debate is about deficit spending: raising spending without raising taxes.

For example, the large fiscal stimulus enacted in 2009 was not "paid for." Yet it has been claimed that it created essentially no jobs. Really? With spending under the Recovery Act exceeding $600 billion (and tax cuts exceeding $200 billion), that would be quite a trick. How in the world could all that spending, accompanied by tax cuts, fail to raise employment? In fact, according to Congressional Budget Office estimates, the stimulus's effect on employment in 2010 was at least 1.3 million net new jobs, and perhaps as many as 3.3 million.

Concerns About Interest Rates and Deficits

A second job-destroying mechanism operates through higher interest rates. When the government borrows to finance spending, that pushes interest rates up, which dissuades some businesses from investing. Thus falling private investment destroys jobs just as rising government spending is creating them.

There are times when this "crowding-out" argument is relevant. But not today. The Federal Reserve has been holding interest rates at ultra-low levels for several years, and will continue to do so. If interest rates don't rise, you don't get crowding out.

In sum, you may view any particular public-spending program as wasteful, inefficient, leading to "big government" or

The Impact of Government Spending

By taking decisive action to address the hemorrhaging of jobs and the fall in economic activity, Congress and the administration actually reduced the deficit, relative to where it would be today had no such action been taken. At the most basic level, government spending reduced unemployment and thus increased tax revenues. The current projected budget deficit for fiscal year 2011 stands at $1.3 trillion. Had Congress done nothing to stop the hemorrhaging of jobs, economists estimate that the deficit would have ballooned to more than twice as large as it actually did, hitting $2.6 trillion in fiscal year 2011.

Heather Boushey and Michael Ettlinger, "Government Spending Can Create Jobs—and It Has," Center for American Progress, September 8, 2011.

objectionable on some other grounds. But if it's not financed with higher taxes, and if it doesn't drive up interest rates, it's hard to see how it can destroy jobs.

Let's try one final argument that is making the rounds today. Large deficits, it is claimed, are creating huge uncertainties (e.g., over what will eventually be done to reduce them) and those uncertainties are depressing business investment. The corollary is a variant of what my Princeton colleague Paul Krugman calls the Confidence Fairy: If you cut spending sharply, confidence will soar, spurring employment and investment.

As a matter of pure logic, that could be true. But is there evidence? Yes, clear evidence—that points in the opposite direction. Business investment in equipment and software has been booming, not sagging. Specifically, while real gross domestic product grew a paltry 2.3% over the last four quarters [April 2010–March 2011] business spending on equipment and software skyrocketed 14.7%. No doubt, there is lots of uncertainty. But investment is soaring anyway.

More Jobs and a Lower Deficit

Despite all this evidence and logic, some people still claim that fiscal stimulus won't create jobs. Spending cuts, they insist, are the route to higher employment. And ideas have consequences. One possibly frightening consequence is that our limping economy might have one of its two crutches—fiscal policy—kicked out from under it in an orgy of premature expenditure cutting. Given the current jobs emergency, that would be tragic.

Yet it is undeniable that we have a tremendous long-run deficit problem to deal with—and the sooner, the better. So it appears we're caught in a dilemma: We need both more spending (or lower taxes) to create jobs and less spending (or higher taxes) to tame the deficit monster. Can we square the circle?

Actually, yes. Suppose we enacted a modest fiscal stimulus program specifically designed for maximum job creation. My personal favorite is a tax credit for firms that add to their payrolls, but there are other options. And suppose we combined that with a serious plan for reducing future deficits—and enacted the whole package now. Then we could, in a sense, have our cake and eat it, too.

A package like that is not fantasy. I believe that a bipartisan group of economists, if given the authority, free of political interference, would design some version of it. But that's not how budget decisions are, or should be, made. And as long as one political party clings to the idea that government spending kills jobs, it's hard to see how we extricate ourselves from this mess. As Keynes understood, ideas, whether right or wrong, have consequences.

Viewpoint 4

> *"Government spending ultimately 'kills jobs' because jobs are not a static commodity to be purchased and put on a shelf."*

Government Spending Kills Jobs

John Hayward

In the following viewpoint, John Hayward argues that government spending eliminates jobs, objecting to the argument of a Keynesian economist who claims otherwise. Hayward contends that government spending skews the true demand of the marketplace, preventing the private sector from creating jobs that are actually needed in the economy. Furthermore, Hayward claims that the deficit spending used to create jobs by the government is unsustainable and will ultimately lead to less job creation in the private sector. Hayward is a staff writer for Human Events.

As you read, consider the following questions:

1. Blinder claims that when Republicans object to government spending for killing jobs, they are talking about what kind of jobs?

John Hayward, "How Government Spending Kills Jobs: It's Time to Put an End to Keynesian Mythology," *Human Events*, June 21, 2011.

2. The author contends that rampant government spending conceals what?
3. Why, according to Hayward, would a tax credit for job creation not be successful in creating jobs?

The *Wall Street Journal* ran an editorial today [June 21, 2011] from Alan Blinder, a professor of economics and public affairs at Princeton University, who also once served as vice chairman of the Federal Reserve. Blinder's piece is provocatively titled "The GOP Myth of 'Job-Killing' Spending," and his goal is to debunk the idea that government spending leads to job destruction. He finds the idea patently absurd.

The Public and Private Sectors

"The claim is that employment actually declines when federal spending rises," explains Blinder. "Using the same illogic, employment should soar if we made massive cuts in public spending—as some are advocating right now."

I hate to rip off Blinder's blinders right at the outset, but when Republicans "rail against job-killing government spending," they're talking about the destruction of *private-sector jobs*. His whole piece, which is remarkably silly for someone who teaches economics, is premised on ignoring that distinction.

Even so, the rest of his argument is pitifully weak. "Even building bridges to nowhere would create jobs, not destroy them, as the congressman from nowhere knows," he sneers, presumably referring to [US] House [of Representatives] Speaker John Boehner, the only congressman he previously named. Does Blinder really not understand that the value lost in transferring huge amounts of money to the public sector, for the construction of unnecessary boondoggles, results in lost job opportunities? What would the people involved in building the "bridge to nowhere" be doing, if they were not being paid in tax dollars to waste their time? Where would the people who coughed up those tax dollars have preferred to invest them?

The Issue of Deficit Spending

Blinder addresses the idea that "taxes necessary to pay for government spending destroy more jobs than the spending creates," but says this would "require extremely inept choices of how to spend the money and how to raise the revenue." Isn't he the one who was just talking about "bridges to nowhere?" Does he not understand the economic impact of the actions taken by potential job creators to avoid high taxes and regulations?

Not to worry, though, because the spending we're all concerned about these days is *deficit* spending, which means nobody had to pay for it, or something. "The large fiscal stimulus enacted in 2009 was not 'paid for,'" Blinder assures us, and yet it created "at least 1.3 million net new jobs, and perhaps as many as 3.3 million."

Don't expect a Princeton professor to look up the actual figures when he's on a roll. For that matter, don't expect the government to produce any reliable figures for him to consult. The performance of the stimulus is always measured with the nonsense "created or saved" metric. Nobody really knows how many jobs the stimulus "created." But by all means, let's give them fresh piles of money and let them create jobs all over the place!

Just for the sake of argument, let's give Blinder the high end of his guesswork, and say the stimulus created 3.3 million jobs. The stimulus money is all spent now. What happens to those jobs? Blinder is very cavalier about rampant deficit spending. Why don't we just blow, say, $10 trillion more, right now, and create jobs for everyone?

The Creation of False Demand

The sad thing about Keynesians is that they remain in a perpetual state of bafflement over the existence of time and motion. Blinder is the kind of academic who puckers his lips over the latest "unexpected" job numbers, and wonders why unemployment is so bad. Let me take a stab at explaining it to him:

Government spending ultimately "kills jobs" because *jobs are not a static commodity* to be purchased and put on a shelf. They are commitments, created in response to demand.

Rampant government spending *conceals demand*. Government subsidies and bridge-to-nowhere projects create false "demand" where none truly exists. The blizzard of imaginary deficit dollars blowing through our economy disrupts the normal feedback mechanisms used by the private sector to detect and exploit opportunity. It's hard to listen for the elusive sounds of profitable demand when a government-funded symphony orchestra fills the air with deafening nonsense.

Diverting free-market resources to the government destroys much of the value from free exchange, which produces robust employment. At the same time, we do not give the State the kind of authoritarian power it would need to actually "put everyone to work," by compelling them to perform jobs assigned by the government, and compensating them as the government sees fit. The environment resulting from such an exercise of power cannot be described as "prosperity." Americans are not hungry for full employment in labor camps.

The Creation of Jobs

Few serious analysts would dispute that the private sector hires, on balance, more people with the same amount of money than the government. Does not transferring control of that money to the government therefore result in a loss of jobs? Or are we supposed to pretend that the crazy deficit spending can go on forever?

Blinder thinks the answer to our unemployment woes, which included double-digit real unemployment despite that job-creating stimulus bomb he praises, would be "a modest fiscal stimulus program specifically designed for maximum job creation." His personal favorite is "a tax credit for firms that add to their payrolls." It's always fun to listen to the ramblings of a Keynesian who thinks a subsidy for wedding rings will lead to more marriages.

Few employers will be strongly motivated to make the long-term commitment of hiring and training new staff, and paying their increasingly costly benefits, because of a little one-time tax credit. Tax credits for new hires do little to stimulate businesses that see no compelling reason to expand. They offer no incentive for entrepreneurs paralyzed by real and threatened government regulations to form new businesses.

Blinder makes a great show of mocking the "illogic" of believing "employment should soar if we made massive cuts in public spending." What say we give it a try, and see how things work out? I'll bet all the fashionable academics will be surprised by the "unexpected" results.

Viewpoint 5

> *"Ten years after the first round of Bush tax cuts were signed into law, we know with certainty that they were a huge mistake."*

The Bush Tax Cuts Have Had a Disastrous Fiscal Impact

Michael Linden and Michael Ettlinger

In the following viewpoint, Michael Linden and Michael Ettlinger argue that the tax cuts enacted in 2001 under President George W. Bush should end. Linden and Ettlinger claim that if the tax cuts had never been passed, there would have been lower deficits each year and a lower overall debt now. The authors claim that in order to stop the economic damage and meet the needs for the future, the Bush tax cuts should be allowed to expire at the end of 2012. Linden is director for tax and budget policy, and Ettlinger is vice president for economic policy at the Center for American Progress.

As you read, consider the following questions:

1. According to the authors, when US president George W. Bush took office the total debt as a share of GDP (gross domestic product) was what?

Michael Linden and Michael Ettlinger, "The Bush Tax Cuts Are the Disaster That Keeps on Giving: Debt Would Be at Sustainable Levels Without Them," Center for American Progress, June 7, 2011. www.americanprogress.org.

2. Linden and Ettlinger claim that if the Bush tax cuts had never been enacted, the total debt as a share of GDP would have stayed below what through 2021?
3. If the Bush tax cuts are extended, the total debt as a share of GDP will rise to what level by 2021, according to the authors?

Ten years ago today [June 7, 2001], the first round of Bush tax cuts became law. But what if they hadn't? What would our fiscal situation look like if history had been different in just one respect: if we'd never implemented President George W. Bush's eponymous tax policies? The short answer is that the debate over federal debt levels would be entirely different. In that alternate world, total debt as a share of GDP [gross domestic product] would be under 50 percent this year—instead of pushing 70 percent—and it would be expected to stay under 60 percent for the rest of the decade. That's well below the levels causing such great consternation in Washington.

The Impact of the Bush Tax Cuts

Bear in mind that President Bush inherited perhaps the strongest federal balance sheet in postwar history. There were record-high surpluses, debt was at around 30 percent of GDP and falling, and the Congressional Budget Office [CBO] projected that the federal government would be debt free by 2009. The country was in great fiscal shape to deal with any crises or emergencies coming down the road, and it was even ready to deal with the coming retirement of the baby boom generation.

But rather than follow President Bill Clinton's successful lead, President Bush handed out gigantic tax cuts, with people at the top of the income ladder getting the biggest breaks. Those "supply-side" tax cuts were a complete failure as economic policy, and now, instead of being debt free and well prepared to care for an aging population, our debt-to-GDP ratio is almost 70 percent. If those tax cuts are extended—instead of being allowed to

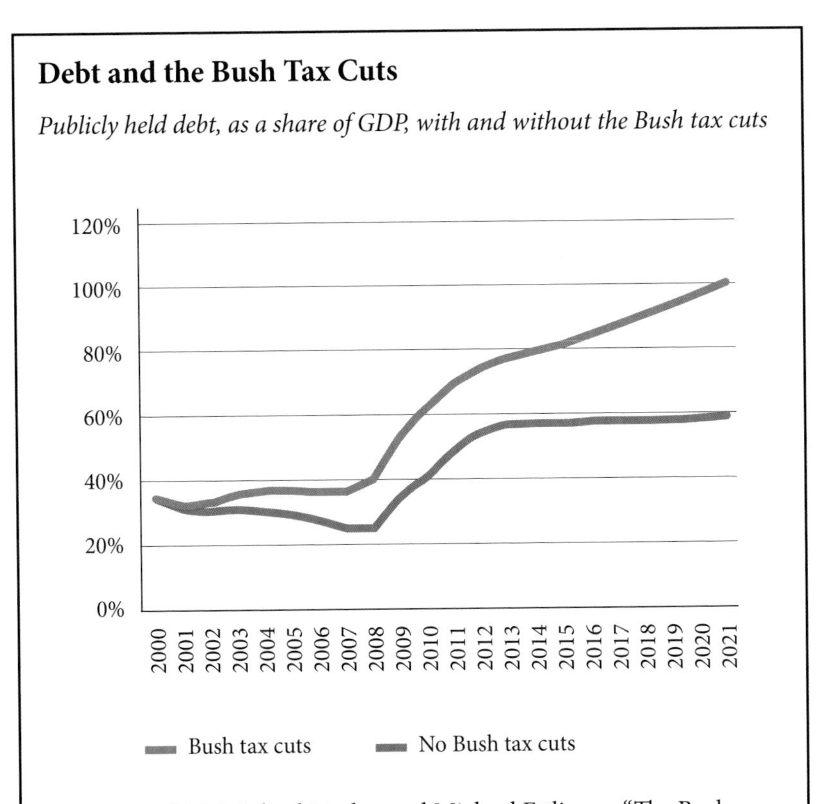

TAKEN FROM: Michael Linden and Michael Ettlinger, "The Bush Tax Cuts Are the Disaster That Keeps on Giving: Debt Would Be at Sustainable Levels Without Them," Center for American Progress, June 7, 2011. www.americanprogress.org.

expire on schedule at the end of 2012—it will approach 100 percent by 2021.

A World Without the Tax Cuts

Of course, other factors contributed to the federal budget's deterioration: the terrorist attacks of September 11, 2001; the subsequent recession; the wars in Iraq and Afghanistan; President Bush's domestic spending programs; and the onset of the Great Recession at the end of 2007, which led to massively reduced tax collections as incomes plummeted.

But even with all of that, when one adds back the foregone revenue from the Bush tax cuts to the actual revenue collections over the past 10 years, the debt picture suddenly becomes markedly better. That additional revenue would have meant lower deficits in each year and therefore lower overall debt. And lower debt means lower interest payments on that debt, further reducing deficits. In the "no Bush tax cuts" alternate universe, our debt-to-GDP ratio would be less than 50 percent this year even after all the other fiscal shocks of the past 10 years.

Similarly, in a future without the Bush tax cuts, the national debt would be under control. In the Congressional Budget Office's official baseline, the debt-to-GDP ratio rises by only 3 percentage points from 2012 to 2021 despite the retirement of the baby boomers. In large part, that's because the CBO baseline assumes the full expiration of the tax cuts. And if instead of starting from almost 75 percent of GDP, we were starting from just 55 percent—which is where we'd be in 2012 if the Bush tax cuts had never happened—debt would stay below 60 percent for the remainder of the decade. There is no magic level above which the debt level becomes dangerous. But few, if any, consider 60 percent of GDP in debt as a significant risk to the country.

The Need to End the Tax Cuts

To some extent, there's nothing we can do about the disastrous fiscal impact of the Bush tax cuts now. We're stuck with the debt built up during the past 10 years, and we're stuck with the interest payments on that debt. But we can make choices about where we go from here.

We know that the next few decades are going to be difficult ones for the federal budget. As the population ages, it will cost more to ensure a safe and secure retirement for America's senior citizens.

So can we afford to continue a tax regime that's already weakened our ability to meet those needs? If all the Bush tax cuts are extended, debt will rise from about 70 percent of GDP this year to just less than 100 percent of GDP by 2021. Debt will reach 93 percent of GDP by 2021 if the bonus tax cuts on income of more than $250,000 are allowed to expire but the rest remain. If we allow all the Bush tax cuts to expire after 2012 as scheduled, debt will be around 80 percent by 2021. [All three scenarios assume that the alternative minimum tax is indexed to inflation.]

There's no undoing the fiscal damage from the Bush tax cuts. But we can learn from the mistakes of the past and try not to repeat them. Ten years after the first round of Bush tax cuts were signed into law, we know with certainty that they were a huge mistake. Without them, the country would have been in much stronger shape to weather all the fiscal storms of the past 10 years and much better prepared for those of the next 10.

> *"If the current administration allows any or all of the Bush tax cuts to expire, economic growth will be slowed and tax revenue could actually decrease, perpetuating our deficit dilemma."*

The Bush Tax Cuts Were Good for Economic Growth

Andrew Foy and Brenton Stransky

In the following viewpoint, Andrew Foy and Brenton Stransky argue that the tax cuts implemented under President George W. Bush have not unfairly favored the rich and have increased government revenue. They contend that the Bush tax cuts increased economic growth and if they are allowed to expire, recovery from the recession will be prolonged. Foy is a medical resident at Thomas Jefferson University Hospital in Philadelphia and a captain in the US Army Reserves. Stransky is a financial consultant. They are co-authors of The Young Conservative's Field Guide.

As you read, consider the following questions:

1. According to the authors, total income tax paid by the top 40 percent of income earners grew by what percent of the total from 2000 to 2004?

Andrew Foy and Brenton Stransky, "Lying About Bush's Tax Cuts," *American Thinker*, March 5, 2010. www.americanthinker.com.

2. Foy and Stransky claim that the data reveals tax revenue in 2006 was above the level projected by how much?
3. The authors support their claim that allowing the Bush tax cuts to expire will harm the economy by drawing an analogy to what historical event?

The majority of the taxpayers in our country believe it a foregone conclusion that taxes will rise substantially in the near future and that the Bush tax cuts will soon be no more than a footnote of political history. You don't need to be a genius to see that the government will have to raise more revenue to pay for seemingly infinite spending, but before we resign ourselves to higher taxes, we should consider defending the Bush tax cuts against the left.

Two of the most oft-cited objections to the Bush tax cuts by the left are that *it helped only the rich* and *it was largely responsible for the federal deficit at the end of the Bush presidency.* Instead, it is true that if the current administration allows any or all of the Bush tax cuts to expire, economic growth will be slowed and tax revenue could actually decrease, perpetuating our deficit dilemma.

The Misconception of Helping the Rich

The Economic Growth and Tax Relief Reconciliation Act of 2001 and the Jobs and Growth Tax Relief Reconciliation Act of 2003 broadly lowered income, capital gains, dividends, and estate taxes. Fanning the lie that only the rich benefited, liberal economists Peter Orszag and William Gale described the Bush tax cuts as reverse-government redistribution of wealth, "[shifting] the burden of taxation away from upper-income, capital-owning households and toward the wage-earning households of the lower and middle classes." This criticism stuck so well that it is difficult to find a liberal today who doesn't believe that these tax relief measures were anything more than "tax cuts for the rich."

But the data does not support this conclusion. According to the non-partisan Congressional Budget Office (CBO), the Bush tax cuts actually shifted the total tax burden farther toward the rich so that in 2000–2004, total income tax paid by the top 40% of income-earners grew by 4.6% to 99.1% of the total.

This shift may have occurred because as the wealthy (who are arguably the most industrious and productive citizens) are better-incentivized to be industrious and productive through lower taxes, they create higher incomes for themselves and end up paying more taxes. The Bush tax cuts did shift the tax burden, but not in the direction most liberals think.

The Misconception About the Deficit

The second major misconception spread by the left about the Bush tax cuts is that the lower tax rates caused the federal deficit woes we face today. Keeping with the party line of blaming the previous administration for all of today's problems, Speaker [of the US House of Representatives] Nancy Pelosi (D-CA) quipped in a news conference on January 8 of this year [2010]: "Let me just say that the tax cuts at the high end . . . have been the biggest contributor to the budget deficit." Of course, the Speaker would have us believe that overspending has nothing to do with our deficit.

In fact, the Bush tax cuts actually *increased* government revenue. According to economist Brian Riedl of the Heritage Foundation, The Laffer Curve (upon which much of the supply-side theory is based) merely formalizes the common sense observations that:

- Tax revenues depend on the tax base as well as the tax rate,
- Raising tax rates discourages the taxed behavior and therefore shrinks the tax base, offsetting some of the revenue gains, and
- Lowering tax rates encourages the taxed behavior and expands the tax base, offsetting some of the revenue loss.

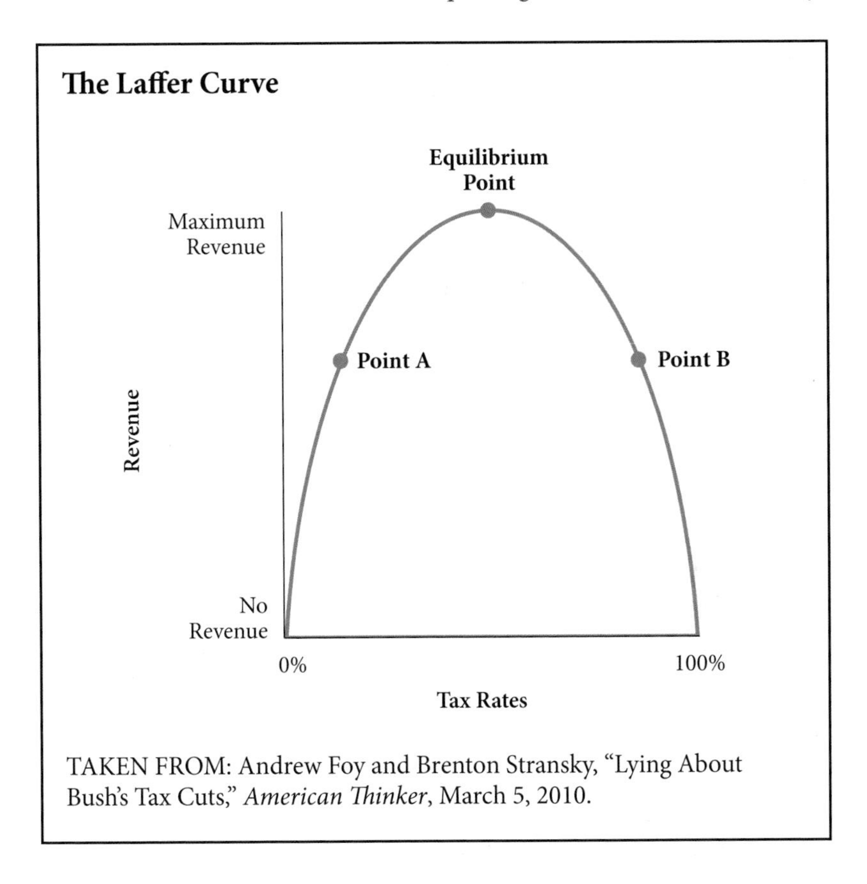

The Laffer Curve

TAKEN FROM: Andrew Foy and Brenton Stransky, "Lying About Bush's Tax Cuts," *American Thinker*, March 5, 2010.

If policymakers intend cigarette taxes to discourage smoking, then they should know that high investment taxes will discourage investment and income taxes will discourage work. Lowering taxes encourages people to engage in the given behavior, which expands the base and replenishes some or all of the lost revenue. This is the "feedback effect" of a tax cut. . . .

The Laffer Curve . . . postulates that two tax rates exist between the extremes of no tax and 100% tax that will collect the same amount of revenue: a high tax rate on a small tax base and a low tax rate on a large tax base. Whether or not a tax cut recovers 100% of the lost revenue depends on the tax rate's location on the Laffer curve. When tax rates are above the equilibrium point on the Laffer curve, reducing the tax rate increases revenue.

So what was the effect of the Bush tax cuts? The data reveals that tax revenues in 2006 were actually $47 billion above *the levels projected* by the Congressional budget office before the 2003 tax cuts. Clearly, tax rates were beyond the point of equilibrium.

The Empirical Data

The Bush tax cuts were intended to increase market incentives to work, save, and invest and thus create jobs and increase economic growth. An analysis of the six quarters before and after the 2003 tax cuts shows that this is exactly what happened. . . .

The empirical data makes it impossible to validate the liberal claims that the Bush tax cuts were "for the rich," or that they "caused the budget deficit," or that they were in any way responsible for causing this latest economic crisis. In fact, a study by economist John W. Skorburg underscores the positive effects of the Bush tax cuts. Skorburg's study found that the Bush tax cuts, which lowered the total federal tax burden from 20.9% in fiscal year 2000 to 17.9% in fiscal years 2008 and 2009, were responsible for increasing the economic growth rate. Further, the author concluded that "[i]f President Obama raises tax burdens, trend growth in real GDP [gross domestic product] will fall."

The bottom line is that tax policy has far-reaching effects, and for decades, liberals have refused to acknowledge them. The dire consequences of higher tax burdens in times of economic weakness were made most clear when FDR [President Franklin D. Roosevelt] raised taxes in 1937, causing a double-dip in GDP that prolonged the Great Depression. If the Bush tax cuts are allowed to expire, recovery from the current crisis will likely be prolonged, and we will have no one to blame but ourselves for not observing the lessons of history.

Periodical and Internet Sources Bibliography

The following articles have been selected to supplement the diverse views presented in this chapter.

Alberto Alesina	"Tax Cuts vs. 'Stimulus': The Evidence Is In," *Wall Street Journal*, September 15, 2010.
Alan S. Blinder and Mark Zandi	"Stimulus Worked," *Finance and Development*, December 2010.
Neal Boortz	"Neal Boortz: Bush Tax Cuts Didn't Create the Deficit," *Atlanta Journal-Constitution*, June 24, 2011.
Tad DeHaven	"The Stimulus: The Government Job Creation Myth," *Richmond Times-Dispatch*, August 1, 2010.
Thomas Donnelly	"Obama Guts Defense: Who Will Speak for National Security?," *Weekly Standard*, April 13, 2011.
Chris Edwards	"Federal Spending Doesn't Work," *Daily Caller*, July 1, 2011.
Andrew Fieldhouse	"Ten Years Later, the Bush Tax Cuts Remain Unfair, Ineffective, and Expensive," Economic Policy Institute, June 6, 2011. www.epi.org.
N. Gregory Mankiw	"Crisis Economics," *National Affairs*, Summer 2010.
Jim Powell	"Why Government Spending Is Bad for Our Economy," Forbes.com, October 13, 2011.
Richard P. Rumelt	"World War II Stimulus and the Postwar Boom," *Wall Street Journal*, July 30, 2011.
Judith Stein	"Keynesian Stimulus Isn't Enough: The Great Recession and the Trade Deficit," *Dissent*, August 25, 2011. www.dissentmagazine.org.
Michael D. Tanner	"Feeling Spent," *New York Post*, September 10, 2011. www.nypost.com.

Chapter 4

How Must Government Spending Change to Meet Future Challenges?

Chapter Preface

According to the US Government Accountability Office (GAO), "Current fiscal policy is unsustainable over the long term." The problem, according to GAO, is the aging population: Absent reform of federal retirement and health programs for the elderly—including Social Security, Medicare, and Medicaid—federal budgetary flexibility will become increasingly constrained. Assuming no changes to projected benefits or revenues, spending on these entitlements will drive increasingly large, persistent, and ultimately unsustainable federal deficits and debt as the baby boom generation retires. With a larger percentage of retirees burdening the system, along with longer life expectancies, spending for retirement and health care of senior citizens is outpacing the ability of the current system.

GAO estimates that without an increase in revenue, by 2030 spending on Social Security, Medicare, Medicaid, and interest paid on the national debt will take up the majority of the annual budget. By 2040, the annual revenue will not even cover the cost of that spending, let alone allow for spending on national defense, transportation, education, or other federal spending programs. There is little dispute that there is a problem, but how to address it is a subject of much disagreement.

Some economists argue that the problem can be resolved by allowing people to manage their own accounts for retirement, disability insurance, and health care insurance. President of the National Center for Policy Analysis, John C. Goodman, says the current system costs too much and delivers too little because "government insurance is monopoly insurance, instead of a service that arose through competition in the marketplace." He points to innovative systems in Singapore and Chile that require citizens to have individual retirement accounts but allow them to manage them. *Reason* editor Nick Gillespie and columnist Veronique de Rugy argue that a primarily private system would still allow a program to help those in need: "It would make more sense to have a system in which individuals who are too poor or sick to take care of themselves would receive financial assistance, but everyone else would be expected to provide for their retirement and health care."

Not everyone critical of current entitlement spending wants to privatize the programs. Economists C. Eugene Steuerle and Stephanie Rennane argue that Social Security and Medicare pay out more to beneficiaries in benefits than those beneficiaries have paid in taxes, claiming "total lifetime benefits consistently outweigh lifetime contributions across a range of scenarios." They contend, "Tax rates in Social Security and Medicare have always been low, while benefits have almost continually increased faster than wages." Steuerle and Rennane suggest the following solutions: higher payroll taxes, more work later in life, or higher premiums for health care for the elderly.

There is no doubt that changes are needed to address the future costs of Social Security, Medicare, and Medicaid. There is no consensus, however, about the proposed solutions. In this chapter, experts debate various challenges to future government spending.

Viewpoint 1

> *"Increasing the EEA for Social Security benefits could encourage Americans to remain in the workforce longer, significantly increasing their retirement income, boosting economic output, and increasing tax revenues."*

The Early Retirement Age for Receiving Social Security Should Be Raised

Andrew G. Biggs

In the following viewpoint, Andrew G. Biggs argues that the Earliest Eligibility Age (EEA) for collecting Social Security benefits should be raised from age sixty-two to age sixty-five. Biggs claims that doing so will lead to increased retirement incomes, a boost to the economy, and increased federal tax revenue. In response to concerns about the raised EEA, Biggs argues that people unable to work to age sixty-five may collect disability insurance. Biggs is a resident scholar at the American Enterprise Institute in Washington, DC, and former principal deputy commissioner of the Social Security Administration.

Andrew G. Biggs, "The Case for Raising Social Security's Early Retirement Age," *Retirement Policy Outlook*, vol. 3, October 2010, pp. 1–5, 7. American Enterprise Institute.

As you read, consider the following questions:

1. According to the author, when the Social Security program was established in 1935, the age of earliest eligibility for benefits was what?
2. Biggs claims that if the Earliest Eligibility Age (EEA) increased to age sixty-five, median Social Security benefits would increase by how much, in 2010 dollars?
3. If the EEA were increased, the number of individuals claiming disability insurance benefits would increase by a factor of what, according to the author?

Increasing the EEA [Earliest Eligibility Age], while of small importance to Social Security's finances, could significantly increase retirement incomes while boosting the economy and federal tax revenues. Some individuals could not work longer due to poor health, but the health status of older Americans has improved significantly while the physical demands of work have declined. The evidence indicates that most Americans could work longer and would benefit from doing so.

The Social Security Early Retirement Age

Three ages are important for claiming Social Security retirement benefits. Age sixty-two is the EEA, commonly known as the early retirement age. The Full Retirement Age (FRA) is currently sixty-six and will move gradually to sixty-seven by the early 2020s. Age seventy is the oldest age at which benefits are increased to account for delayed claiming; there is generally no reason to delay claiming after age seventy. Social Security benefits increase by around 7 percent for each year an individual delays claiming after age sixty-two, although the exact schedule differs by age.

When the Social Security program was established in 1935, the age of earliest eligibility and the normal retirement age were both sixty-five. In other words, there was no provision for early retirement. In practice, most individuals claimed benefits *later* than age sixty-five; in the 1950s, for instance, the average age of first benefit claiming was sixty-eight. At the time, Social Security had a strict earnings test, such that the receipt of even a small amount of earnings disqualified individuals from receiving benefits. In response, individuals generally waited until they were fully withdrawn from the labor force before claiming Social Security.

However, in response to concerns that some individuals could not work until age sixty-five, the Social Security Amendments of 1956 (for women) and 1961 (for men) allowed for early claiming at age sixty-two, with a reduction in benefits. In response to this change, the average age of initial benefit claiming declined by two years from 1960 to 1970, from 66.2 to 64.2. The average claiming age as of 2007 was 63.6 for men and 63.5 for women.

Labor-force participation rates for older males also declined from the mid-1950s through the mid-1990s in response to the availability of Social Security benefits at earlier ages, although other factors also contributed to this change. Rising incomes may reduce retirement ages, as individuals take part of the income gain in the form of leisure. Rising life expectancies, by contrast, may promote longer work lives as individuals offset the cost of supporting themselves in longer retirements. A number of other factors come into play, including physical and mental job requirements, the demand for older workers, and policy incentives regarding the retirement decision. For decades after World War II, the trend was toward falling labor-force participation at older ages and earlier claiming of Social Security benefits. While benefit-claiming ages remain low, over the past two decades labor-force participation among older individuals has risen, suggesting that forces promoting longer work lives may be having an effect. Some older individuals who might have left the workforce before claiming Social Security are now remaining at work, while other older individuals are continuing to work even after claiming retirement benefits. Labor-force participation rates for women rose over the same period, as part of a broader shift from working at home to paid employment, partially offsetting lower labor-force participation by men.

The Age of Initial Benefit

By far the most common age of initial retirement benefit claiming is sixty-two, when 42 percent of men and 48 percent of women claim benefits. The next most common age is sixty-five; this is driven both by the FRA long having been sixty-five and by the availability of Medicare benefits at that age. The FRA is currently sixty-six and gradually rising to sixty-seven; the norming effects of the FRA as well as the reduction in benefits associated with an increased retirement age may produce somewhat higher claiming ages. . . . The average age of benefit claiming has remained relatively steady since 1970. With the exception of 1997, when the average age spiked to 64.5, average claiming ages have tended to vary by only a few decimal points from year to year.

The increase in the FRA for Social Security implies a 13 percent reduction in monthly benefits if individuals do not respond by delaying benefit claiming. For this reason, some have proposed increasing the EEA along with the FRA. Raising the EEA from sixty-two to sixty-five may seem like a steep increase but would only bring the United States in line with other developed nations. In Canada, the Old Age Security pension is available at age sixty-five. The United Kingdom's Basic State Pension can be claimed at age sixty-five for men, with claiming as early as sixty for women. However, claiming ages for women are being increased to match those of men, and ages for both genders will gradually be increased to sixty-eight over the next four decades. Likewise, New Zealand's Superannuation benefits begin only at age sixty-five.

The Effects of Increasing the EEA

Using a suite of models from the Policy Simulation Group (PSG), I simulate the effects of increasing the EEA from sixty-two to sixty-five on the Social Security program, individual re-

Initial Social Security Claims

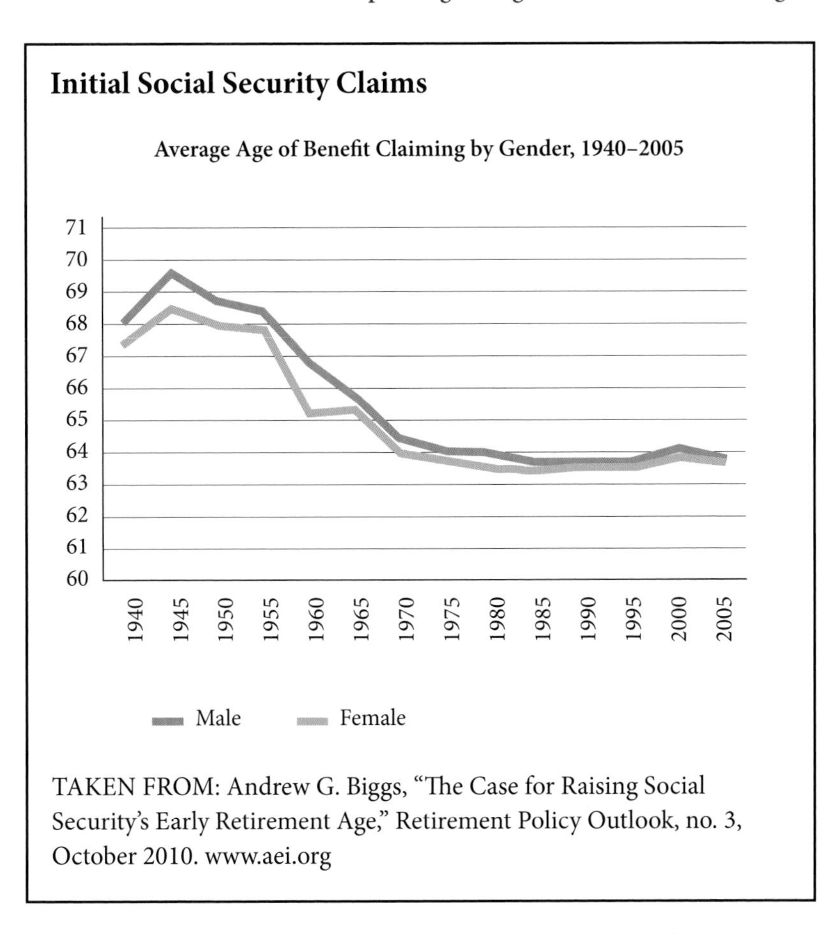

TAKEN FROM: Andrew G. Biggs, "The Case for Raising Social Security's Early Retirement Age," Retirement Policy Outlook, no. 3, October 2010. www.aei.org

tirement income, and the economy. The PSG models are used by the Government Accountability Office, the Social Security Administration, and the Department of Labor to simulate the effects of policy changes on Social Security and private pensions. These models can provide a detailed view of how an increased EEA would affect Social Security's financing, how individuals would be affected by the changes, and how the economy might react to increases in the labor force.

The policy change I simulate is a gradual increase in the EEA from sixty-two to sixty-five over the period from 2015 to 2025. Current retirees would be unaffected, but the change would be phased in for individuals born between 1952 and 1960. Other variations are possible, and this exercise is intended merely to provide a feel for the results. No other changes are made to Social Security policy, though other changes will be necessary to make the program solvent over the long term.

Social Security's finances would be largely unchanged by an increase in the EEA. The long-term deficit, which is 1.92 percent of taxable payroll under the 2010 Social Security Trustees Report, would rise to about 1.93 percent of payroll. The life of the Social Security trust fund would be extended by around five years, from 2037 to 2042.

While not inconsequential, these effects are modest. The reason, as noted above, is that Social Security increases benefits in response to delayed retirement. Under current law, if individuals delayed claiming benefits from age sixty-two to sixty-five, their monthly checks would rise by about 20 percent. Moreover, raising the EEA would increase benefits by an additional 3.5 percent because of how Social Security benefits are calculated. Thus, Social Security's financing profits from the extra taxes many individuals would pay if forced to delay retirement, but the gains to solvency are modest due to increased benefits paid out.

The Effects on Retirement Incomes

An increase in the EEA may be perceived as merely a forced delay in retirement, and in many respects it is. Monthly Social Security benefits are increased by about 8 percent for each year that benefits are delayed, plus an inflation adjustment that averages around 3 percent. In addition, however, a little-known facet of the Social Security benefit formula would provide a small additional increase to benefits, such that total lifetime benefits would increase by about 6 percent.

But because higher lifetime Social Security benefits would be consumed over a shorter retirement, gains to individual retirement incomes from increasing the EEA would be significant. Social Security benefits paid at age seventy to individuals in the

1980 birth cohort would increase by an average of 17.1 percent. In addition, average income derived from defined contribution and defined benefit pensions would increase by 15.1 percent due to longer work lives in which savings would be amassed and shorter retirements in which savings would be drawn down. Combined, total Social Security and private-pension incomes would increase by 16.1 percent. Median annual Social Security benefits would increase by around $4,300, and median annual total Social Security plus pension income would increase by around $7,500, in constant 2010 dollars.

Another way of measuring retirement-income adequacy is through replacement rates, which represent retirement income as a percentage of preretirement earnings. Financial advisers generally recommend a replacement rate of 70 to 80 percent of preretirement earnings, although individual needs vary significantly. Under current law, the median couple in the 1980 birth cohort will receive a total Social Security benefit equal to 43 percent of preretirement earnings. Adding pension income raises total replacement rates to 67 percent of preretirement earnings. Mean values would be somewhat higher. On top of Social Security and pensions, households may rely on personal savings and other sources of income, so these should not be considered complete measures of retirement-income resources.

Increasing the EEA to age sixty-five would raise the median Social Security replacement rate from 43 to 51 percent of preretirement earnings. The median combined Social Security and pension replacement rate would rise from 67 to 77 percent, making a significant dent in the percentage of individuals considered ill-prepared for retirement. Only around 6 percent of households in the bottom third of the earnings distribution would have replacement rates below 70 percent, with 4 percent having replacement rates below 60 percent. Given that most households, including low-income households, have limited resources beyond Social Security and employer-sponsored pensions, the share of low earners who would retire with inadequate replacements would be significantly reduced under this policy.

Moreover, when replacement rates are adjusted for household size and composition, both baseline rates and rates after increases in the EEA are significantly larger. Simple replacement-rate measures can misstate a household's preparation for retirement by ignoring how the costs of raising children and economies of scale in household size can affect retirement-income needs. Adjusting for these factors raises median baseline Social Security replacement rates by around 12 percentage points and would have similar effects on replacement rates after increasing the EEA. If retirement-income needs are properly measured, increasing the EEA would generate total incomes that make a large majority of households well-prepared for retirement. In fact, increasing the EEA may be the single most effective policy for raising total retirement income, as it would boost both Social Security benefits and pension savings.

The Effects on the Economy and Tax Revenues

While increasing the EEA would not resolve Social Security's financial challenges, the economy would benefit due to a larger workforce. To the degree that individuals continue to work, their earnings would contribute to both GDP [gross domestic product] and federal tax revenues.

The PSG models estimate that raising the EEA would increase long-run GDP by about 5.5 percent, meaning that in future years economic output would be around 5.5 percent higher than it would be with a lower Social Security eligibility age. Increases in GDP would differ from year to year based on factors such as changes in the age structure of the population, the national saving rate, and the reaction of other workers' wages to changes in the labor force. Nevertheless, these results highlight the significant potential economic impact of greater labor-force participation among near-retirees. This increase in output, equivalent to around $800 billion annually in current terms, would improve Americans' standards of living and provide extra resources with which to address long-term budget shortfalls.

Based on these projections of changes in GDP, over the 2015–2024 period non–Social Security federal revenues would increase by about $1.2 trillion in nominal dollars. This estimate derives from the percentage of GDP collected under the Congressional Budget Office's "alternative budget scenario" in which most of the 2001 and 2003 tax cuts would be retained. Revenue increases would be larger over the longer term, as the projected increase in GDP over the first ten years of implementation averages only 2.4 percent versus a long-term increase of around 5.5 percent.

By comparison, raising the EEA would improve the federal budget over ten years by almost six times as much as is projected for the recent health reform bill. Over the period 2010–19, the Congressional Budget Office projects that health reform will improve the annual budget balance by an average of 0.08 percent of GDP; over the first ten years of increasing the EEA, from 2015 to 2024, the federal budget balance would improve by about 0.45 percent of GDP. While these new revenues are nowhere near sufficient to address the long-term budget gap, they are a very strong start.

The Ability to Work Longer

It is reasonable to counter that Americans cannot work longer—and many Americans cannot. While the physical strains of work have been reduced as the United States has shifted toward a service and technology economy, in today's marketplace declining analytical and social skills may impose larger obstacles to work than physical strength. But these obstacles to longer work lives can be overcome. If an increase in the EEA is considered, a number of policies could reduce stresses on more vulnerable individuals.

If the EEA were increased, individuals who could not work would not be prohibited from claiming Disability Insurance benefits in the years from age sixty-two to sixty-five. These individuals would receive benefits payable as of the FRA of sixty-six or sixty-seven and thus would not suffer a financial penalty if forced to leave the workforce due to disability. Simulations using the PSG models show that almost twice the number of individuals would claim Disability Insurance benefits between age sixty-two and sixty-five, a figure that appears consistent with academic work on the subject. While rising disability costs are a significant part of Social Security's long-term funding shortfall, increased disability claims by older workers are an inevitable, and legitimate, offshoot of an increased EEA. The Disability Insurance program provides a safety net for individuals who truly cannot work longer.

To provide additional protections for vulnerable workers, the eligibility age for Supplemental Security Income (SSI) for the elderly could be lowered from sixty-five to sixty-two. SSI is a means-tested welfare program that provides benefits to the elderly, as well as the blind and the disabled. In 2010, the maximum monthly federal SSI payments are $674 for individuals and $1,011 for couples. In addition, most states provide additional payments on top of SSI to eligible individuals. Lowering the SSI eligibility age would protect low-income individuals who did not qualify for disability benefits.

But even without these extra protections, we should not overestimate the barriers to delayed retirement. One of the best pieces of evidence that delayed retirement is possible is that it has been done in the past, when work conditions were more strenuous and health conditions poorer than they are today. While policy should be designed to protect those who cannot delay retirement due to poor health or other factors, policy should also recognize that individuals who cannot work longer are the exception rather than the rule. . . .

Increasing the EEA for Social Security benefits could encourage Americans to remain in the workforce longer, significantly increasing their retirement income, boosting economic output, and increasing tax revenues. Extended work lives are possible for most Americans and would generate significant benefits to the economy, the federal budget, and, most importantly, individuals' own retirement security.

"While raising the retirement age is problematic, the need for Social Security is greater than ever."

The Retirement Age for Receiving Social Security Does Not Need to Be Raised

David Rosnick

In the following viewpoint, David Rosnick argues that although life expectancy has grown, the eligibility age for collecting Social Security benefits does not need to be increased. Rosnick claims that extra savings are needed to pay for lengthier retirements, and he says this should be met by reducing the trade deficit. Furthermore, he contends that increased national savings for Social Security will not be experienced as a lowered standard of living because of the increased productivity of future generations. Rosnick is an economist at the Center for Economic and Policy Research in Washington, DC.

As you read, consider the following questions:

1. According to the author, by how many years has life expectancy increased for men and women since 1899?

David Rosnick, "Social Security and the Age of Retirement," Center for Economic and Policy Research, June 2010. www.cepr.net.

2. The average number of years a twenty-year-old man could expect to work by age sixty-five rose by how many years between 1899 and 1949, according to Rosnick?
3. The author claims that the Congressional Budget Office projects the cost of Social Security will rise by what percent of gross domestic product (GDP) from 2010 to 2083?

The last century has seen large increases in life expectancy for both men and women. A man born in 1899 could expect to live 51.0 years, but a man born fifty years later could expect to live to age 72.9. Similarly, women born in 1899 could expect to live 57.8 years while those born a century later could expect to live to age 84.8.

The Way Social Security Works

Unlike a century ago, people can expect their children to live past the age of retirement. This fact has important implications for how workers save for retirement, but has no specific implications for the retirement portion of Social Security. In addition, the increase in life expectancy is not nearly as important as it might first appear. A significant part of the increase in life is between birth and age 20. Including declines in child and teen mortality exaggerate the increase in retirement length. Furthermore, much of the gains in life expectancy come during working years—between age 20 and retirement. This means that workers are not only experiencing longer retirements, but longer working lives as well. Finally, each succeeding generation has been vastly more productive than prior generations—a trend that will continue. Thus, not only do workers experience, on average, more years of work over their lifetime, they are also better able to save for their retirements.

There is nothing magical about Social Security that provides a free lunch. Workers somehow must pay for longer retirements one way or another. At the same time, there is nothing magical about private savings either. The fact that workers are living longer means they must save more in order to provide for themselves

Expected Years of Life

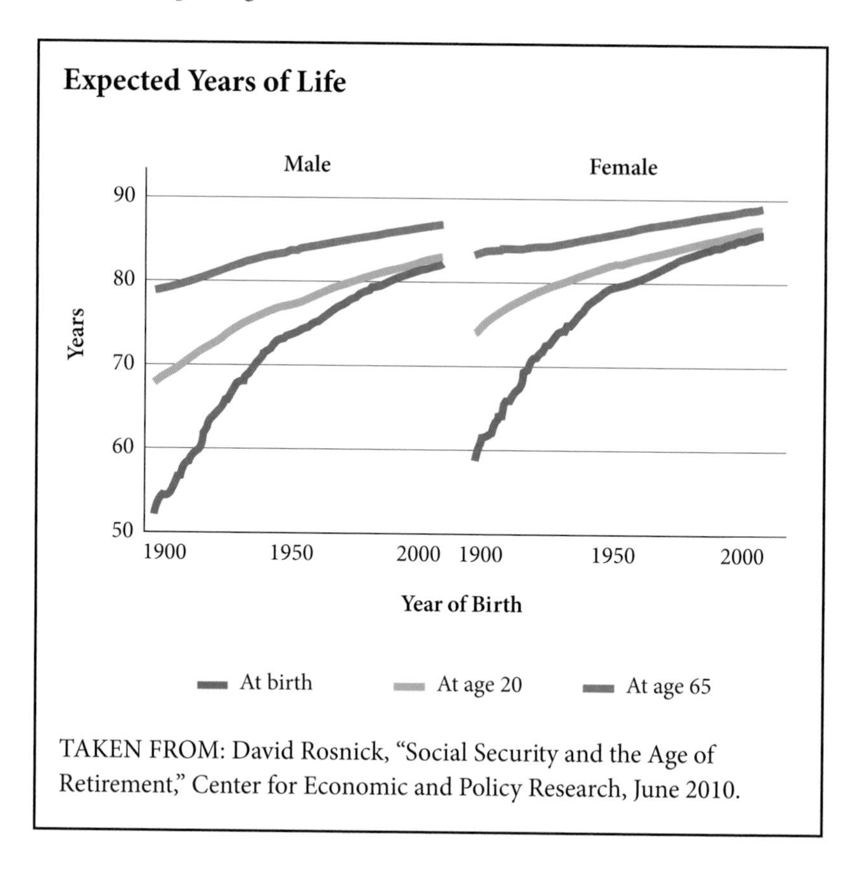

TAKEN FROM: David Rosnick, "Social Security and the Age of Retirement," Center for Economic and Policy Research, June 2010.

later in life—whether they save as individuals or through a program like Social Security. . . .

The savings rates are different if a worker saves as an individual rather than collectively. If an entire cohort of 20-year-old men in 1919 begins pooling savings equal to 6.4 percent of income, then in 1964 the survivors will have just enough money to fully replace their incomes upon retirement. If the individuals try to save individually, each must save 9.3 percent of income.

By itself, this is not to imply that group savings is more efficient—a cohort of savers contributes at a lower rate simply because those who survive claim the savings of those who do not. As 20-year-olds are increasingly likely to live to age 65, the difference in savings rates narrows over time. However, individuals attempting to annuitize their savings in the private sector face charges of 15 to 20 percent. . . .

But for the annuitization fee, the savings rates would turn out to be exactly equal. The difference in required savings rates aside, retirement at age 65 necessitates a higher rate of savings over time. This is true for private savers as well as Social Security. . . .

Life Expectancy and Retirement

Life expectancy improves both with each generation and as each cohort ages. A male born in 1899 could expect to live to age 51.0, but a 20-year-old male in 1919 could expect to live all the way to age 67.3 and at age 65 (in 1964) could expect to live to age 78.5.

The first half of the twentieth century saw extraordinary gains in the life expectancy at birth (for men, nearly 22 years; for women, nearly 21 years). But such improvements did not translate directly into longer retirements. Life expectancy at age 65 for men increased less than five years over this time; for women, about half that amount.

Thus, life expectancy at birth is not an accurate indicator of how workers' retirements have been extended over time. A better indicator is the expected length of retirement for 20-year-olds. . . .

While life expectancy at birth rose 22 years for men, a young adult in 1969 could expect a retirement only 5.5 years longer (13.8 years) than a 20-year-old in 1919 (8.3 years.) In part, this is due to the increase in the retirement age from 65 to 66. For women, the increase in the retirement age was more meaningful, as their life expectancy increased by less than it did for men. In fact, women born in 1960 could, at age 20, expect a retirement of 17.1 years—one month longer than the expected retirement of women born in 1937 despite more than two extra years of life expectancy.

At first blush, one might think that increasing retirement lengths should require an increase in the normal retirement age. However, increases in life expectancy lengthened the average number of working years as well as years of retirement—even when holding the retirement age at 65. . . .

The average number of years a 20-year-old man could expect to work by age 65 rose from 39.0 to 42.0 between those born in 1899 and those born in 1949. Raising the retirement age to 66 added another ten months to the average working life. Those born in 1999 will average 45.0 years of work before retirement age. Even under current law, the younger generations will work considerably longer than generations of workers past.

For many, these additional years of work needed to reach normal retirement age will be a considerable burden. While an investment banker, economist or senator may find it a small thing to delay retirement two more years, the same cannot be said for coal miners, auto workers, and janitors. Life expectancy may increase, but that doesn't mean a firefighter ought to keep working at age 66 or 68 or beyond.

Alternatives to an Increase in the Retirement Age

While raising the retirement age is problematic, the need for Social Security is greater than ever. With the collapse of the stock market bubble at the turn of the millennium and the more recent bursting of the real estate bubbles, workers have lost a large share of their meager savings. Many workers effectively made highly leveraged bets that their home price would continue to rise. They were led to believe that these bets were a sure thing by their own real estate agents, media outlets that celebrated the rise in house prices, and the economics profession that denied the existence of a housing bubble. By making the mistake of following the advice of the experts, many workers lost most or all of their savings when the price of their homes fell rather than rose. Consequently, they need stable and secure retirement income more than ever. Instituting cuts in Social Security (directly, or in the form of raising the retirement age) in the face of a crisis in savings would destroy any hope of a secure retirement for the baby boomers.

On the other hand, national savings must be increased. As we saw above, savings rates must increase over time in order to provide for longer retirements. Historically, this has been the case within Social Security. Congress has raised the OASI [Old Age and Survivors Insurance] tax rate many times—in the 1950s, 1960s, 1970s, 1980s, and 1990s. Yet there is no evidence that these members of Congress have suffered when it came time for reelection. Outside of Social Security, though, the rate of private savings has fallen in recent decades.

Only with the recent economic crisis and the resulting increase in the government budget deficits have private savings begun to recover. The relationship between public dissaving and private savings follows from the savings-investment accounting identity:

[Savings − Investment = (Government Expenditures − Taxes) − (Imports − Exports)] $S - I = (G - T) - (M - X)$

For a given level of investment, a large trade deficit (broadly defined) requires some combination of large budget deficits and low private saving. To increase national savings, then, requires a reduction in the trade deficit. The trade deficit, in turn, is driven by an overvalued dollar that makes imports to the United States relatively inexpensive and exports from the United States more expensive. In effect, an overvalued dollar is akin to a tariff on exports and a subsidy on imports.

The Impact of Increased Savings

Finally, it is not true that increased savings (as opposed to delayed retirement) requires a reduction in the standard of living. Productivity has and—by all projections—will increase with each generation. Each succeeding generation will be wealthier and more productive than the previous. For example, the Congressional Budget Office [CBO] projects that the cost of Social Security will rise from 4.8 percent of GDP [gross domestic product] in 2010 to 6.2 percent in 2083—an increase of about

1.5 percentage points. On the other hand, over those same 73 years, CBO projects that real GDP will increase 2.3 percent *per year*—a combined 426 percent.

If we take the extra cost of Social Security out of future income, then the burden is equivalent to reducing real GDP growth from 2.30 to 2.28 percent per year. Rounding error will have more impact on projections of future income than will paying for Social Security.

Since the introduction of Social Security, life expectancy has grown, but much of the gains have taken the form of increased time spent working. For women in particular, the increase in working years means that they will see a length of retirement virtually the same as their parents. For those who labor in more physically demanding areas of the economy, working to an even later age is not a serious option. Fortunately, future generations will be far more productive than today—hence able to afford the lengthy retirements that increased life expectancy offers. While paying for these longer retirements does require additional savings on the part of workers, this is no less true in retirement planning generally than it is for Social Security. Thus, there is a need to increase national savings; but this requires addressing America's persistent trade deficits—not denying seniors retirement income.

> *"If government bought green, it would drive down marketplace prices sufficiently that the momentum toward green tech would become self-reinforcing and spread to the private sector."*

Government Spending on Clean Energy Should Be Increased

Christian Parenti

In the following viewpoint, Christian Parenti argues that the best way for government to help develop clear energy is to reorient government procurement to clean energy. Parenti claims that the government can help create a market for affordable green energy because it is able to buy large quantities, which will drive prices down and close the clean-tech price gap. Rather than investing in innovation or attempting to impose unpopular mandates, he concludes that using existing purchasing power is the best green investment. Parenti is an investigative journalist and author of Tropic of Chaos: Climate Change and the New Geography Violence.

Christian Parenti, "The Big Green Buy," *Nation*, vol. 291, no. 5–6, August 2–9, 2010.

As you read, consider the following questions:

1. According to Parenti, how many buildings and vehicles does the federal government own or lease?
2. The US Defense Department uses what percentage of the total energy that the federal government consumes, according to the author?
3. Parenti claims the building stock of the General Services Administration (GSA) is already how much more efficient than the private sector?

In the wake of the BP oil spill, some captains of industry have begun calling for government leadership to spur a clean-energy revolution. In June [2010] billionaire software mogul Bill Gates visited Washington and encouraged lawmakers to pony up public subsidies to triple clean-tech R&D [research and development] funding from $5 billion to $16 billion annually. Gates explained to the *Washington Post* that much of what is touted as free-market innovation was born of government subsidies: "The Internet and the microprocessor, which were very fundamental to Microsoft being able to take the magic of software and having the PC explode, were among many of the elements that came through government research and development." And on his website Gates wrote, "When it comes to developing new sources of energy, and ways to store that energy, I believe the federal government needs to play a more active role than it does today."

Innovation and Implementation

Gates's acknowledgment of the need for government intervention is welcome, but he and many others are stuck on "innovation." The fixation on new "game-changing" technology is omnipresent. Think of the metaphors we use: a green Manhattan Project or a clean-tech Apollo Program. It recalls [French historian Alexis de] Tocqueville's observation that "the American lives in a land of wonders, in which everything around him is in constant movement, and every movement seems an advance.

Consequently, in his mind the idea of newness is closely linked with that of improvement."

Yet according to clean-tech experts, innovation is now less important than rapid large-scale implementation. In other words, developing a clean-energy economy is not about new gadgets but rather about new policies.

An overemphasis on breakthrough inventions can obscure the fact that most of the energy technologies we need already exist. You know what they are: wind farms, concentrated solar power plants, geothermal and tidal power, all feeding an efficient smart grid that, in turn, powers electric vehicles and radically more energy-efficient buildings.

But the so-called "price gap" is holding back clean tech: it is too expensive, while fossil fuels are far too cheap. The simple fact is that capitalist economies will switch to clean energy on a large scale only when it is cheaper than fossil fuels. The fastest way to close the price gap is to build large clean-tech markets that allow for economies of scale. So, what is the fastest way to build those markets? More research grants? More tax credits? More clumsy pilot programs?

The Big Green Buy

No. The fastest, simplest way to do it is to reorient government procurement away from fossil fuel energy, toward clean energy and technology—to use the government's vast spending power to create a market for green energy. After all, the government didn't just fund the invention of the microprocessor; it was also the first major consumer of the device.

Call it the Big Green Buy. The advantage of this strategy is that it is something [President Barack] Obama can do right now, without waiting for Congressional approval to act. As such, it amounts to a real test of his will to make progress in the fight against climate change.

Consider this: altogether, federal, state and local government constitute more than 38 percent of our GDP [gross domestic product]. Allow that to sink in for a moment. The federal government will spend $3.6 trillion this year [2010]. In more concrete terms, Uncle Sam owns or leases more than 430,000 buildings (mostly large office buildings) and 650,000 vehicles. The federal government is the world's largest consumer of energy and vehicles, and the nation's largest greenhouse gas emitter. Add state and local government activity, and all those numbers grow by about a third again.

A redirection of government purchasing would create massive markets for clean power, electric vehicles and efficient buildings, as well as for more sustainably produced furniture, paper, cleaning supplies, uniforms, food and services. If government bought green, it would drive down marketplace prices sufficiently that the momentum toward green tech would become self-reinforcing and spread to the private sector.

The Growth in Green Procurement

The good news is that despite our sclerotic, largely right-wing Congress, government agencies are turning toward procurement as a means to jump-start clean tech and cut emissions.

Perhaps the most important move in this direction came in October 2009, when President Obama quietly signed Executive Order 13514, which directs all federal agencies to "increase energy efficiency; measure, report, and reduce their greenhouse gas emissions from direct and indirect activities; conserve and protect water resources through efficiency, reuse, and stormwater management; eliminate waste, recycle, and prevent pollution; leverage agency acquisitions to foster markets for sustainable technologies and environmentally preferable materials, products, and services; design, construct, maintain, and operate high performance sustainable buildings in sustainable locations."

The executive order also stipulates that federal agencies immediately start purchasing 95 percent through green certified programs and achieve a 28 percent greenhouse gas reduction by 2020. The stimulus package passed in 2009 included $32.7 billion for the Energy Department to tackle climate change, and some of that money is now being dispersed to business and federal agencies.

Already some federal agencies are installing energy management systems and new solar arrays in buildings, tapping landfills to burn methane and replacing older vehicles with plug-in hybrids and soon some all-electric vehicles. But it is the green procurement part of the executive order that is most interesting.

Government has tremendous latitude to leverage green procurement because it requires no new taxes, programs or spending, nor is it hostage to the holy grail of sixty votes in the Senate. It is simply a matter of changing how the government buys its energy, vehicles and services. Yes, in many cases clean tech costs more up front, but in most cases savings arrive soon afterward. And government—because of its size—is a market mover that has already shown it can leverage money-saving deals.

The Clean-Tech Price Gap

Currently, the price gap relegates clean tech to boutique status: San Francisco [SF] Mayor Gavin Newsom owns an electric car; SF City Hall has three electric-vehicle charging stations; nationwide there are about 55,000 electric vehicles and 5,000 charging stations. Groovy.

However, back on Planet America the asphalt transportation arteries are clogged with 250 million gasoline-powered vehicles sucking down an annual $200–$300 billion worth of fuel from more than 121,000 filling stations. Add to that the cost of heating and cooling buildings, jet travel, shipping, powering industry and the energy-gobbling servers and mainframes that are the Internet, and the US energy economy reaches a spectacular annual tab of $2–$3 trillion.

The clean-tech price gap is partly the result of old dirty tech's history of subsidies ($72.5 billion between 2002 and 2008), but it is also the result of the massive economies of scale that the fossil fuel industry enjoys. In other words, gas pumps and gasoline are cheaper when you buy in bulk.

Closely associated with the price gap is another concept, which clean-tech developers call the "valley of death." This is the time in a technology's life cycle when capital dries up, the time between a technology's initial invention and its successful application as a moneymaking commodity.

A report by [professional service organization] Ernst & Young found that a typical technological innovation—like the flatscreen TV or the cellphone—costs about $20–$100 million to invent but about $1 billion to deploy at competitive prices. Between government subsidies and capital markets, there is often enough financing available to invent new gadgets or buy into a mature and profitable business. But there is a dearth of capital for new companies trying to cross that gap between victory in the lab and victory in the market.

The Impact of Large Orders

Smith Electric Vehicles of Kansas City [Missouri] is one company that would benefit immensely if government started robust green procurement. Currently Smith, the US affiliate of a British firm that has been making electric delivery trucks for eighty years, turns out about twenty units a month. The vehicles—flatbeds, refrigerator trucks, basic box-style delivery trucks—all require components that Smith buys on the open market.

"If we could buy gear boxes in batches of a hundred rather than ten at a time, they could be cast to our specifications rather than each one machined. That would immediately cut the cost by 30 to 40 percent," says Smith CEO Bryan Hansel. Similar savings would be available for other inputs like steel chassis, cabs, drive shafts, suspensions and wiring harnesses, all of which are purchased from the same suppliers used by diesel- and gas-powered vehicle makers.

In March Smith received a $32 million Energy Department grant that will help it offset the cost of its trucks. But what would really give it a boost is an order of 1,000 trucks a year for the next ten years, from, say, the Defense Department [DoD] or the Postal Service or the General Services Administration (GSA). If that happened, Smith's plans to open twenty more small manufacturing facilities around the country would shift into high gear.

"We have approached the DoD about nontactical vehicles, like trucks that are used on bases here in the US. They bought four of our vehicles for testing. So we're hopeful," says Hansel. The Defense Department has 160,000 nontactical vehicles, many of which are suitable for electrification.

In other respects, the military is one of the most avid adaptors of clean technology. Of all the energy the federal government consumes, 80 percent is used by the Defense Department. The cost of delivering fuel to forward operating areas can be as high as $400 a gallon, by some estimates. And according to an Army Environmental Policy Institute report, 170 soldiers died and many more were horribly maimed just protecting fuel in combat zones during 2007. For purely strategic reasons the military is trying to free itself (at least a bit) from its clumsy and very long fossil fuel tether.

Thus the military is experimenting on a large scale with green technology. Fort Irwin, in California, is building a 500 megawatt (that is big) solar power plant and is on track to become self-sufficient in electricity use within a decade. Fort Leavenworth is undergoing an energy retrofit that a Pew report described thus: "energy efficiency improvements are made by a private-sector firm at no upfront cost to the Army, with resulting savings shared by the base and the contractor." The list goes on, but unfortunately most of the changes are relatively small scale.

Laws to Increase Green Procurement

Government procurement, particularly the military's, would become significantly greener if two recently introduced bills became law. The Department of Defense Energy Security Act of 2010, introduced by Gabrielle Giffords of Arizona [reintroduced in 2011 and referred to committee], would require the department to derive a quarter of its electricity from renewable sources by 2025. And—good news for Smith Electric Vehicles—the bill also calls, rather ambitiously, for a full-scale conversion of the military's nonradical vehicle fleet to electric, hybrid or alternative-fuel vehicles by 2015.

A similar bill, introduced by Democrat José Serrano of New York [and referred to committee], would require the Postal Service [USPS] to purchase at least 20,000 electric vehicles by 2015. That goal is reasonable, and the USPS is a perfect place to start, as most of its vehicles travel in loops of less than 20 miles each day and always park in the same garage. Thus, even current battery technology is sufficient. Many other government fleets fit the same profile: they have regular routes of less than 100 miles a day and use the same parking spot each night, so they are easy and cheaper to charge because the price of juice drops at night.

Right now a vehicle from Smith is about 20 percent more expensive than a standard gas or diesel truck. But the cost per mile to run an electric truck is about one-third the cost per mile of a gas- or diesel-powered one. Hansel says that with enough large orders his product will reach cost parity with dirty-tech options. When that happens, large private-sector fleets, like UPS, FedEx, Staples and Frito-Lay, will start buying electric vehicles [EVs], simply because it will be the cheaper option.

In anticipation of that day, Nissan is releasing the 2011 Leaf, a fully electric plug-in car. It plans to make 90,000 of them. Chevy is coming out with the Volt—10,000 of them. Will this first generation of EVs really have a market, and sufficient charging options? Who knows? But you can be sure they would if Big Government made the Big Green Buy.

The General Services Administration

Buildings also use lots of energy. The US Green Building Council reports that buildings account for about 36 percent of America's total energy use and emit roughly the same proportion of greenhouse gases. But if properly constructed and managed, many buildings could actually generate energy for their own use, for vehicles or to put back into the grid.

The government's building manager—its janitor, if you will—is the GSA. The GSA constructs, repairs and manages federal buildings; it buys the supplies and keeps the heat and AC on; and it buys and maintains much of the government's nonmilitary vehicle fleet. It also acts as a purchaser and contractor of sorts for most other federal agencies. The GSA is about as dull an agency as you can imagine. It has pocket-protector and brown shoes written all over it. But in the age of climate change, its brief has taken on vital importance. The implications of Executive Order 13514 have put the GSA, along with the military, at the cutting edge of the Big Green Buy.

"We're taking this very seriously," says Martha Johnson, administrator of the GSA. "We are normally sort of overlooked, but we were thrilled, really excited, when the president gave us such prominent place in his environmental strategy."

President Bill Clinton issued four executive orders on sustainable clean procurement, but they lacked specific targets or enforcement mechanisms and thus achieved very little. "Our progress in general in buying these products stinks," said Dana Arnold, senior program manager at the White House Office of the Federal Environmental Executive in a recent interview with the *Federal Times*.

This time it may be different, and the GSA is gearing up to be the point agency in what is sometimes called Environmentally Preferable Procurement, or "green supply chain management." The GSA is putting up solar arrays, buying a few electric cars and hybrids, trying to produce energy at its buildings and buying renewable energy like biomass, solar and wind power, which now account for 10.8 percent of the GSA's federal building power supply. It is also creating monitoring systems to track progress and keep federal agencies accountable.

The GSA's sustainability plan requires "a minimum of three percent renewable energy source for all competitive electricity supply contracts and requires that renewable energy be from a plant that was recently built in order to stimulate greater investment in the industry." The agency has reduced its own energy use by 15 percent, as measured against a 2003 baseline, and plans to reduce energy consumption in its buildings by 30 percent from that baseline by 2020. Already the GSA's building stock—mostly offices—is about 22 percent more efficient than similar private-sector buildings.

In addition, the GSA is working on cutting the amount of jet travel its workforce requires and, when possible, increasing telecommuting and home-based work. It is also pressuring other agencies to shut off unused data centers—the USDA [US Department of Agriculture], for example, uses only between 10 percent and 20 percent of its total computing capacity, but its huge, largely empty servers run at 100 percent of power.

Other federal agencies, however, are lagging far behind. "It is amazing to us to find out the low level of awareness," says Linda Mesaros, a consultant for sustainable purchasing. State and local governments are also moving toward green procurement, but few have been very aggressive or ambitious. . . .

Four Green Options

Viewed broadly, there are four simple things the government can do to help close the clean-technology price gap and aid clean-tech business across the valley of death.

First, it can boost R&D as Gates has requested, but that alone won't bring mass-scale green power on line.

Second, it can set up a Green Bank tasked with financing clean-tech businesses as they cross the valley of death. Along with loans, the government can offer more loan guarantees, which encourage otherwise frightened private capital to invest in clean-energy start-ups. The Waxman-Markey climate bill of last year included language to do that, but nothing like it is yet law.

Third, the government can impose mandates on the private sector requiring companies to adopt electric vehicles, purchase clean energy and conserve energy. Industry already lives with numerous rules that put limits on the anarchy of production. Yet in the crazy world of American politics circa 2010, forcing green procurement mandates on business would be very difficult.

So let's get real. The fourth path is the best: a robust program of green procurement is the most immediate and politically feasible thing government can do to boost the clean-tech sector. And the only number that approaches the scale of the energy economy is government spending on energy. We need to be talking not about millions or billions but trillions of dollars going in a new direction. If the government is serious about electric vehicles—then just buy them already!

At one level, the mad Tea Partyers are correct: government is leviathan—a monster. But it is our monster, and with proper leadership even this government in the current climate could jump-start a clean-energy revolution.

VIEWPOINT 4

> *"All subsidies to the electric power sector divert money that would otherwise be invested in higher value wealth and job-creating activities."*

Government Investment in Clean Energy Will Harm the Economy

Ronald Bailey

In the following viewpoint, Ronald Bailey argues that many of the proponents of investment in green energy do not take into account the harmful effects of government policies that invest in clean energy. Bailey claims research shows there is little evidence that such investment will result in more jobs and, in fact, there is evidence that such investment destroys jobs. Bailey worries that government investment diverts money that could have been invested to create more wealth and jobs. Bailey is the science correspondent for Reason *magazine and Reason.com, where he writes a weekly science and technology column.*

Ronald Bailey, "The Unseen Consequences of 'Green Jobs': Will Investing in Clean Energy Harm the Economy?," *Reason*, February 8, 2011. http://reason.com.

As you read, consider the following questions:

1. The author disputes a claim that employment in California's green core economy grew at what rate between 2008 and 2009?
2. The author points to a study finding that the United States currently has how many green jobs?
3. Bailey claims that in the worst cases, investing a million dollars into solar power destroys how many jobs compared to the general investment?

In his State of the Union speech a couple of weeks ago [January 25, 2011], President Barack Obama planned to "win the future" by, among many other things, having the federal government "invest" in "clean energy technology—an investment that will strengthen our security, protect our planet, and create countless new jobs for our people." But will investing in clean energy actually produce countless new jobs?

The Claim About the Green Economy

A couple of weeks ago, the California think tank Next 10 asserted in its *2011 Many Shades of Green* report that employment in the state's green core economy grew at 3 percent between 2008 and 2009. Employment in the rest of the economy, meanwhile, grew at just 1 percent. The report defines the "green core economy" as businesses that generate clean energy, conserve energy, or reduce and recycle wastes.

Specifically, the Next 10 report finds that the number of jobs in California's green core economy rose between 2008 and 2009 from 169,000 to 174,000—an additional 5,000 jobs. Green jobs account for just 0.9 percent of California's overall 18.8 million jobs. Note that California's unemployment rate is 12.5 percent, which means that 2,270,000 Californians are without work.

Unfortunately, when it comes to green jobs both the president and the Next 10 report are focusing on the *seen* while ignoring the *unseen*. In his brilliant essay, "What is Seen and What is Unseen," 19th century French economist Frederic Bastiat pointed out that the favorable "seen" effects of any policy often produce many disastrous "unseen" later consequences. Bastiat urges us "not to judge things solely by *what is seen*, but rather by *what is not seen*."

The Issue of Green Jobs

So let's take a look. Many of the green core economy jobs created in California are the result of policies that restrict the production and use of conventional sources of energy. For example, electricity generators in California are required to produce 20 percent of their supplies using renewable sources by 2010, a requirement that will rise to 33 percent by 2020. In addition, California's Global Warming Solutions Act will impose steep reductions in carbon dioxide emissions produced by burning fossil fuels. Other green jobs are the result of regulations requiring energy conservation in residential and commercial construction. Certainly, these activities provide some benefits, including pollution reduction and energy savings. But let's focus on the claim that on balance they provide more jobs than they kill.

A new report, "Defining, Measuring, and Predicting Green Jobs," by University of Texas economist Gurcan Gulen, issued by the Copenhagen Consensus Center, takes apart many studies predicting that policies mandating alternative energy production, energy efficiency, and conservation will create a boom in employment.

First, Gulen notes that many such studies fail to define clearly what they mean by green jobs. He points out that many pro-green jobs studies do not distinguish temporary construction jobs from more permanent operation jobs. Many studies also assume that green jobs will pay more than jobs in conventional energy production. But why would a construction job at a wind farm pay more than one at a conventional power plant?

Even more disturbingly, many green job studies have no analyses of job losses. Clean energy costs more than conven-

The Supposed Jobs Benefit

Alternative energy technologies, energy efficiency and conservation and other environmentally friendly programs have benefits ranging from lower emissions to enhanced energy security, albeit at different levels for different technologies or approaches. But adding "net jobs" cannot be defended as another benefit of investing in these technologies. Models can be developed to analyze alternative scenarios that can show net job gains over a certain period of time but these are based on aggressive and unrealistic assumptions of continuous and fast technological innovation, rapid progression of economies of scale, global implementation of similar green policies, adoption of protectionist measures such as tariffs or local content requirements and others.

Gurcan Gulen, "Defining, Measuring, and Predicting Green Jobs," Copenhagen Consensus Center, February 2011. www.copenhagenconsensus.com.

tional energy, which means consumers and businesses will have less income with which to buy and invest. This reduces their consumption of other goods and services, resulting in job losses in those sectors—one of Bastiat's "unseen" effects. In addition, many studies simultaneously count on protectionist policies to exclude clean energy imports while assuming that domestic companies will be freely exporting to other countries.

A Questionable Strategy

As an example of how these pro-green jobs studies go wrong, Gulen analyzes the 2008 green jobs study by the consultancy IHS Global Insight. That report found that the U.S. currently has

750,000 green jobs, of which 420,000 are in the engineering, legal, research, and consulting fields. Gulen observes, "Given that there are also categories for renewable generation, manufacturing, construction, and installation, it is likely that the majority of the jobs in the largest category are not directly associated with the generation of a single kWh (kilowatt-hour) of 'green' power or a single Btu (British thermal unit) of 'green' fuel." The Global Insight study also reports that government administration generates 72,000 of the current green jobs. Green policies often don't produce power, but do produce more regulators.

The Global Insight study further asserts that pursuing green energy will increase economic productivity. "When compared to conventional technologies on unit of energy output, due to intermittency and low capacity factors, wind and solar are likely to be more labor intensive (hence less productive)," notes Gulen. In fact, Gulen adds that other studies are counting on the fact that green energy technologies are more labor intensive as a way to generate more jobs.

This strategy is reminiscent of the no doubt apocryphal story of the American economist visiting [Communist leader] Mao's China taken on a tour of a construction site where 100 workers were using shovels to build an earthen dam. "Why don't you just use one man and a bulldozer to build the dam?" asked the economist. The guide responded, "If we did that, then we'd have 99 men out of work." To which the economist replied, "Oh, I thought you were building a dam. If your goal is to make jobs, why don't you take their shovels away and replace them with spoons?"

A Shift of Investment

Gulen is not alone in his concerns about overblown claims for green jobs. A 2009 report, by Hillard Huntington, executive director of the Energy Modeling Forum at Stanford University, also found that promoting green energy is not a jobs generator. Huntington calculated the number of jobs per million dollars invested in various types of electricity generation. A million dollars invested in solar power produces three to five jobs; wind 1.6 to 6.5 jobs; biomass 1.8 to 6.5 jobs; coal 3.7 jobs; and natural gas two jobs. It looks like renewables are often winners at job creation until Huntington points out that on average an investment of a million dollars produces about 10 jobs.

"Electricity generation across all sources creates far fewer jobs than other activities in the economy; the estimates in the figure suggest that they range between 17–67 percent of the average job-creation in the economy," reports Huntington. "These net job losses mean that subsidies to either green or conventional sources will detract rather than expand the economy's job base, because they will shift investments from other sectors that will create more employment."

Another way to look at it is that in the worst cases, investing in solar power destroys seven jobs, wind eight jobs, biomass eight jobs, coal six jobs, and natural gas eight jobs, each compared to the 10 jobs generally created per million dollars of investment. All subsidies to the electric power sector divert money that would otherwise be invested in higher value wealth and job-creating activities.

Huntington concludes, "Policymakers and government agencies should look askance at the claimed additional job benefits from green energy." Gulen agrees, "Adding 'net' jobs cannot be defended as another benefit of investing in these [green] technologies." In other words, President Obama and other proponents of green energy like Next 10 are seeing only what their policies produce, and ignoring what their policies destroy.

> *"Congress needs to find the courage to go beyond the trite neoconservative cliches and actually make cuts in the wasted projection of American military power abroad."*

Defense Spending Should Be Cut

Thomas R. Eddlem

In the following viewpoint, Thomas R. Eddlem argues that US spending on defense should only include what is necessary. He claims that neoconservative resistance to cuts in defense spending stems from an unjustified view of the United States as the world's policeman, which Eddlem argues is a financial burden that is not good for US security. Eddlem is a writer and high school history teacher in Massachusetts.

As you read, consider the following questions:

1. According to Eddlem, defense spending costs each US household approximately how much per year?
2. How much was spent on the wars in Iraq and Afghanistan, according to the Congressional Budget Office estimate cited by the author?

Thomas R. Eddlem, "Can We Cut 'Defense' Spending?," *New American*, March 8, 2011. www.thenewamerican.com.

3. According to the author, the United States has approximately how many military personnel deployed abroad as of September 2010?

Andrew Ferguson of the *Weekly Standard* summed up the neoconservative case against cutting U.S. defense spending in a February 21 [2011] article entitled "The Stockman Temptation." In Ferguson's article, he recollected that President [Ronald] Reagan's Budget Director David Stockman had told Reagan back in the early 1980s that he must cut the defense budget in order to balance the budget. "Defense is not a budget issue," Reagan responded. "You spend what you need."

The Definition of Necessary Spending

Reagan's statement revealed both an undeniable truth as well as the essential question on the appropriate level of defense spending. Nobody who believes in nationhood would argue that the nation shouldn't spend what it needs to defend the territory and citizens of the United States; without that defense spending we would soon no longer have a nation at all. On the other hand, only the economically ignorant would argue that unnecessary spending on armaments and soldiers would be anything but a tragic drag on the economy.

The essential part of Reagan's statement was the word "need." The United States now spends 54 percent of the money expended worldwide on defense, according to the Swedish-based Stockholm International Peace Research Institute's 2010 yearbook, i.e., *more than the rest of the world combined.* In real dollars, that's approximately $1 trillion per year in defense/security programs, once Defense Department outlays, the cost of the Iraq and Afghan Wars, and security spending in other federal agencies (such as Homeland Security, State, Energy, HHS [US Department of Health and Human Services], and intelligence) are included. It's a cost of nearly $9,000 per household in the United States every year.

Thus, with America in a budget crisis, many people are beginning to ask the essential questions:

- How much spending do we really *need?*
- Does the nation really need to spend more than the rest of the whole world combined to be safe, or is spending only more than the three or four next biggest spenders on defense enough?
- Can the United States leverage its uniquely advantageous global geographic position—isolated from much of the world by two oceans—to spend a little less than the next biggest spender?

A Bipartisan Proposal

One odd pair of Congressmen has decided the U.S. government can be safe and still spend a little less on defense: Representatives Ron Paul (R-Texas) and Barney Frank (D-Mass.). Last summer [2010] Paul, arguably the most conservative Congressman in Congress, and Frank, arguably the most liberal, proposed more than $100 billion in cuts in the defense budget for each of the next 10 years, partly based upon scaling back American troop commitments to Europe and some other foreign bases. The two noted that though the United States provided security for Europe and Korea during the Cold War when the two regions were impoverished from war, it's time to pull our troops out. The two argued in the capital-based periodical *The Hill*: "Sixty-five years later, we continue to play that role long after there is any justification for it. . . . The nations of Western Europe now collectively have greater resources at their command than we do, yet they continue to depend overwhelmingly on American taxpayers to provide for their defense." Frank and Paul argue that this defense spending no longer fulfills a defensive "need" for protecting American citizens and their property. Some of their suggested savings include:

- $80 billion: Reduce troops in Europe and Asia by 50,000 (one-quarter of the total);
- $147 billion: Roll back Army and Marine Corps growth as wars in Iraq and Afghanistan end;
- $176.6 billion: Reduce U.S. navy fleet to 230 ships and retire two (of 11) aircraft carriers;
- $157 billion: Cut or eliminate weapons systems—the F-35 Joint Strike Fighter, MV-22 Osprey, kC-X Tanker, and Expeditionary Fighting Vehicle—and cut $50 billion in research;
- $113.5 billion: Reduce the U.S. nuclear arsenal; cancel the Trident II missile program; retire 1,000 deployed warheads, seven Ohio-class SSBNs (ballistic missile submarines), and 160 Minuteman missiles;
- $81 billion: Trim nuclear weapons and space missile defense spending;
- $120 billion: Reduce personnel costs by reforming military pay and healthcare systems;
- $100 billion: Require commensurate savings in command, support, and infrastructure as military is reduced.

One might criticize the Paul-Frank commission because it appears to be heavily based on cutting weapons programs, and one can reasonably argue about which weapons programs should or should not be cut. What's not debatable is that if the United States closes its bases abroad and follows [President] George Washington's advice "to steer clear of permanent alliances with any portion of the foreign world," both equipment costs and costs related to the number of personnel would automatically be greatly reduced. For example, the Paul-Frank proposal expects to save only $147 billion over 10 years from winding down the Afghan and Iraq War troop commitments. But this is only a small part of the savings that could be achieved. President [Barack] Obama's 2012 budget proposal calls for $164.5 billion to be spent in 2011 alone for those two wars, which is close to the average annual cost of the wars according to the Congressional Budget Office [CBO]. The CBO estimated in September 2010 that the total cost of the two wars was more than $1.1 trillion. Why the huge cost? Because the bullets and bombs that are being exploded during the wars have to be replaced. The cost of purchasing such armaments for the unnecessary Iraq War (or in the case of Afghanistan, the *no longer* necessary war) is wasted. And new bombs must be purchased, often at a cost of millions of dollars per bomb.

U.S. "defense" spending today has all of the hallmarks of every other out-of-control big-government program. For example, nobody can say for sure precisely how much the United States spends on defense, and nobody can say for sure how many bases the U.S. government has abroad. Investigative reporter Nick Turse searched official government reports and found that different agencies disagreed with each other over the number. "According to the Department of Defense's 2010 Base Structure Report, the U.S. military now maintains 662 foreign sites in 38 countries around the world," Turse wrote for CBSNews.com on January 10. "Dig into that report more deeply, though, and Grand Canyon-sized gaps begin to emerge." For example, the official roster lists no bases in Kuwait, Saudi Arabia, and Qatar—nations that the United States uses as staging areas for its wars in Iraq and Afghanistan. Ditto for Afghanistan, even though it's known we have more than 400 bases there to wage our war in that troubled nation. Turse eventually concluded that determining the number of U.S. military bases abroad was impossible: "[In] a world where all information is available at the click of a mouse, there's one number no American knows. Not the president. Not the Pentagon. Not the experts. No one."

The Defense of Defense Spending

Despite the potential savings and regardless of U.S. debt, neoconservatives have led the charge against any defense spending cuts, and reacted angrily to the Paul-Frank proposal. A trifecta of neoconservative dons, Ed Feulner of the Heritage Foundation, Arthur Brooks of the American Enterprise Institute, and William Kristol of the *Weekly Standard*, published an opinion piece in the October 4, 2010 *Wall Street Journal* entitled "Peace Doesn't Keep Itself," arguing against Paul and Frank (without naming them): "Military spending is not a net drain on our economy. It is unrealistic to imagine a return to long-term prosperity if we face instability around the globe because of a hollowed-out U.S. military lacking the size and strength to defend American interests around the world."

The key word in the quote by these three neoconservative giants is "interests." By American "interests," they don't mean merely protecting the property and citizens of the United States. The three neocon dons see a world under U.S. hegemony, a world where America is not one independent nation among many, but rather a nation whose prosperity depends upon constant foreign wars and occupations to defend our limitless "interests." The U.S. government, in their worldview, is literally the policeman of the world. And in that world, every spot on the globe—no matter how remote from American soil—is a "vital national interest" for Americans at home that must be controlled with a constant outpouring of blood from American servicemen and treasure from American taxpayers. They continue:

> Global prosperity requires commerce and trade, and this requires peace. But the peace does not keep itself. The *Global Trends 2025* report, which reflects the consensus of the U.S. intelligence community, anticipates the rise of new powers—some hostile—and projects a demand for continued American military power. Meanwhile we face many nonstate threats such as terrorism, and piracy in sea lanes around the world. Strength, not weakness, brings the true peace dividend in a global economy.

Neoconservatives see a world of vague, frightening "threats" against which Americans can only be protected by increased military spending and more projection of "continued American military power" abroad. The vague threats, from pirates to terrorists to unnamed "hostile" nations that may or may not emerge in the future, sound a lot like the search for a threat as an excuse to continue military spending in the classic 1995 comedy movie *Canadian Bacon*. In the film, the U.S. President (played by Alan Alda) is looking for a threat to keep up arms production after the break-up of the Soviet empire, and asks, "What are we going to do for an enemy now?" After his National Security Council plays a slide show presentation featuring old and deceased international bad guys such as [Iranian leader] Ayatollah Khomeini, [Chinese leader] Mao Tse-tung, [Vietnamese leader] Ho Chi Minh, [Soviet Union leader] Leonid Brezhnev, the President exasperatingly remarks: "These guys are all dead. What, are you working from an old list?" But then he adds: "Is this the best you could come up with? What about, you know, international terrorism?" The President's Chairman of the Joint Chiefs replies: "Well, sir, we are not going to reopen missile factories just to fight some creeps running around in exploding rental cars, are we?"

Of course, this is precisely what happened in the real world, largely because terrorists achieved a lucky strike (for them) on September 11, 2001. In the movie, the President and his sniveling advisor Stu Smiley (played brilliantly by Kevin Pollak) decide to portray Canada as a dire "threat" to the United States, despite the President's misgivings. "The American people, Mr. Smiley," the President argues, "would never, ever buy this." But Smiley simply replies: "Mr. President, the American people will buy whatever we tell them to. You know that."

The fictitious world presented by *Canadian Bacon* is essentially the same pitch being made by neoconservatives today. They contend that even though the United States spends more than the rest of the world on defense combined, we are nevertheless threatened to such an extent that we must not only continue shouldering the mammoth military budget we have now, but must also preemptively intervene in myriad "hot spots" throughout the world. To make the case for global empire, they are selling the line of vague "threats," expecting us to believe whatever scare tactics they employ.

The World's Policeman

But the United States does not really need many (if any) bases abroad to project power; we have 11 U.S. Navy carrier battle groups for that. A single carrier battle group could easily handle any of the "nonstate threats such as terrorism, and piracy" that neoconservative leaders claim to fear. Moreover, a single carrier group could easily reduce any Middle Eastern nation to radioactive trinitite glass with the nuclear weapons in its arsenal if necessary. Even without foreign bases, the United States does not lack power to project overseas when needed.

But carrier groups are inadequate for military occupations of foreign countries or for acting as the global policeman, a role the U.S. military has increasingly played under the neoconservative Bush administrations (father and son) and the leftist/interventionist Clinton and Obama administrations. For example, the U.S. military established AFRICOM, a military command for Africa (except Egypt) in 2007. According to the first deputy to the commander for military operations, Vice Adm. Robert Moeller (Ret.), the responsibilities of this command "include piracy and illegal trafficking, ethnic tensions, irregular militaries and violent extremist groups, undergoverned regions, and pilferage of resources. This last challenge includes oil theft, as well as widespread illegal fishing that robs the African people of an estimated $1 billion a year because their coastal patrols lack the capacity to find and interdict suspicious vessels within their territorial waters and economic exclusion zones." In other words, the U.S. military is engaging in Africa as the continental police force. Moeller claims that the United States is keeping a light troop "footprint" in Africa, stressing that headquarters for the command is still based in Germany. But back in 2002 the United States opened up its first major African base in Djibouti, Camp Lemonnier. Moreover, AFRICOM's budget has increased more than 400 percent, up to $310 million for fiscal year 2009 from just $75.5 million a year earlier.

Whether the United States should be policeman of the world is what the defense budget battle is all about. The United States has nearly 400,000 military personnel deployed abroad in more than 100 countries as of September 2010, according to Defense Department statistics. The global commitment of the U.S. military has not only engendered a huge financial burden for American taxpayers, and a tremendous strain on military families, it has also created wide anti-American sentiment around the world. The U.S. military abroad has sparked anti-military protests by thousands in Okinawa, South Korea, and Italy. Even Osama bin Laden claimed he switched his jihad from fighting the atheistic former Soviet Union to the United States only after the U.S. military established permanent bases in the Islamic holy land of the Arabian peninsula. Unlike carrier battle groups, American military bases on foreign soil create an effect known as "blowback," generating the same kind of attacks against Americans that they are nominally erected to protect against.

But the neoconservative movement is not satisfied with the United States minding its own business in international affairs, as George Washington advised in his farewell address. "The United States and the world paid a severe price for the ostrich-like behavior too many democratic nations exhibited during the 1920s and 1930s. Reps. Paul and Frank appear determined to repeat this mistake," Alvin S. Felzenberg and Alexander B. Gray argued in the January 3 [2011] edition of the neoconservative *National Review*. Their column entitled "The New Isolationism" revealed their preferred tactic: comparing anyone who wants less defense spending with those who coddled Hitler before World War Two. Neoconservatives today ask the same question as the President in *Canadian Bacon*: "What are we going to do for an enemy now?" And, amusingly enough, they can't settle on one. There is no Hitler in position today, nor do the *National Review* writers present in their article any but minor (and highly unlikely) threats to U.S. territory that could be handled by a small amount of military power.

Congress needs to find the courage to go beyond the trite neoconservative clichés and actually make cuts in the wasted projection of American military power abroad.

> *"For less than a nickel on the dollar of US GDP, we can maintain our preeminence in the world."*

Defense Spending Should Not Be Cut

Gary Schmitt and Tom Donnelly

In the following viewpoint, Gary Schmitt and Tom Donnelly argue that it would be a mistake to cut the US defense budget. Schmitt and Donnelly claim that high levels of military spending are necessary to preserve the global international order built by the United States, because the United States has a responsibility to defend its homeland, guarantee safe access to the global commons, and achieve a favorable balance of power across Eurasia. Schmitt is director of Advanced Strategic Studies and Donnelly is director of the Center for Defense Studies at the American Enterprise Institute (AEI).

As you read, consider the following questions:

1. According to the authors, defense spending in 2010 was what percent of the budget?
2. Schmitt and Donnelly claim the United States must guarantee safe access to the global commons, which includes what four components?

Gary Schmitt and Tom Donnelly, "The Big Squeeze: The Obama Administration's Defense Budget Portends Strategic Decline," *Weekly Standard*, vol. 15, no. 36. June 7, 2010.

3. The authors criticize the Obama administration's National Security Strategy for emphasizing what three tools?

On the 65th anniversary of the [World War II] Allied victory in Europe in early May [2010], Secretary of Defense Robert Gates spoke at the Eisenhower Library in Abilene, Kansas. His speech was not about America's unprecedented, massive marshalling of resources, men, and materiel to defeat the forces of fascism that threatened to overwhelm the West. Instead, its underlying message was ultimately one of strategic retreat—signaling his and the Obama administration's view that the richest country in the world can no longer afford to sustain the military's current force structure and capabilities.

The Increase in Defense Spending

Channeling his inner President [Dwight D.] Eisenhower, Gates sought to make this message sound not only reasonable but morally justified by belittling Washington, the town where he has spent most of his career. Pandering to those on the left who always see defense spending as dangerous, he raised anew Eisenhower's overwrought concern about the creation of a "garrison state" and a "military-industrial complex." Pandering to those on the right who see the Pentagon as a gigantic sink hole for tax dollars, he dredged up the old saw about the Pentagon being a "Puzzle Palace" and stated that "the attacks of September 11, 2001, opened a gusher of defense spending."

The secretary—along with the Obama administration—wants Americans to believe there is no choice but to cut the defense budget given economic and fiscal realities. Just as there is no crying in baseball, however, there are no inevitabilities in politics. The administration is indeed squeezing defense spending more and more tightly, but that is a product of decisions made and policies chosen. They can and should be revisited.

Speaking of gushers, compare for a moment the size of the Obama stimulus package in 2009—nearly $800 billion—with the more than $300 billion Gates has already *cut* from the Pentagon's budget and the planned "flat-lining" of defense expenditures in the years ahead. And while the secretary talks about cutting overhead by getting rid of unnecessary generals and consultants, the administration has been busy hiring tens of thousands of new federal workers. Gates himself wants to add some 30,000 to the Pentagon's rolls to oversee military acquisitions. Surely, civil servants are not needed more than additional Marines or soldiers, given the back-breaking pace of deployments in recent years and continued overuse of the National Guard and reserves. And who in the administration or congressional leadership is arguing for tough love when it comes to so-called nondiscretionary spending (Social Security, Medicaid, Medicare, and service on the debt)? Right now, those programs cost three times as much as defense, and by the end of a two-term Obama administration they will cost closer to five times as much.

Defense spending has gone up. But never in our history have we fought wars of this magnitude as cheaply. Take, for example, the percentage of the federal budget allocated to defense: In 1994, two years after the collapse of the Soviet Union, Pentagon spending amounted to slightly more than 19 percent of the budget; in 2010, it is the same. And if the administration has its way, that figure will drop to 15.6 percent by 2015. Is any other part of the federal budget getting similarly whacked?

The budget increases that have occurred, moreover, are largely tied to fighting the wars. When [President] Bill Clinton left the White House and [Vice President] Dick Cheney told the military that "help [was] on the way," the defense burden stood at 3 percent of GDP [gross domestic product]—a post-World War II low. When [President] George W. Bush headed out the door, the figure for the core defense budget was about 3.5 percent. This is an increase, to be sure, but not one to make the military flush after a decade of declining budgets and deferred procurement.

The Reality of Military Infrastructure

In his speech, Gates stated that the U.S. military has more than 3,200 tactical combat aircraft—an impressive number. What he did not mention is that the vast majority of the planes have been flying for years, were designed decades ago, and are supported by a tanker fleet that first entered the force six years before Barack Obama was born. Critically, fewer than 150 of these combat aircraft are top-of-the-line, stealthy F-22s, production of which has been capped at 187. Yet even this number doesn't quite capture how limited the force is. Consider the F-22s needed for training, the dispersal of the remaining number among various bases, and the reality that for every plane on station there are two or three in queue, and you get a sense of just how few air-dominance planes we might have on hand during a crisis.

Gates also noted that the U.S. battlefleet is larger than the next 13 navies combined. True. But what he didn't say is that the current number of ships in the fleet, 286, is substantially below the minimum set by several previous studies of what the Navy requires to carry out all the tasks it is charged with around the world. Nor does he mention that this number is shrinking—and will shrink, if the budget stays as is, to levels not seen since the early 20th century. Undoubtedly, the ships of today are far more combat-capable than those of even 15 years ago. Still, numbers matter. Typically, for every ship on station there is one being refurbished after deployment and one undergoing training and work-up prior to deployment. Add to that the fact that the Navy is needed virtually everywhere—protecting the sea lanes, providing support for the wars, gathering intelligence, acting as a missile defense shield, and helping deter the likes of Iran, China, and North Korea—and one quickly comes to appreciate why a much smaller fleet, more widely dispersed, will become a strategic problem.

The tightening of the budget is also going to squeeze the Army. Putting aside the all-important fact that it precludes expanding the active-duty force, a flat or shrinking budget will also

The Cost of Defense

The cost of preserving America's role in the world is far less than would be the cost of having to fight to recover it or, still greater, the cost of losing it altogether. While many Americans would prefer to see our allies and partners play a larger part in securing the blessings of our common liberty, no president of either political party has backed away from America's global leadership role—a bipartisan consensus that remains strong evidence that American leadership is still necessary to protect the nation's vital interests.

American Enterprise Institute,
Heritage Foundation, and Foreign Policy
Initiative, "Defending Defense: Setting the
Record Straight on US Military Spending
Requirements," October 2010.
www.defensestudies.org.

affect what equipment soldiers deploy with in future operations. Because the Army has been fighting in Iraq and Afghanistan, much of its equipment, especially helicopters and vehicles, has been chewed up by wear, tear, and combat. In the past, supplemental appropriations for the war effort helped meet replacement needs; the current administration, however, has halved that funding this year, requiring the Army to begin scrambling to find money in existing and future programs to cover costs.

None of the above means that there are not efficiencies to be found in the way the Pentagon does business, or that there is no need to get a handle on military health care and personnel costs. A good portion of the rising cost per serviceman, however, is connected to the realities of an all-volunteer force now in its fourth decade. In short, there is no magic reform wand that is going to make the Pentagon whole and healthy given the prevailing mismatch between defense dollars and American global strategy. Making the Pentagon 5 percent more efficient—a target any student of public administration would say is about as optimistic as one could be—will lessen but not solve this problem.

The Global International Order

The challenge is to preserve the global international order built and guaranteed by the United States. Though Americans seem habitually averse to thinking strategically, we have actually behaved in a broadly consistent manner since the end of World War II, including the uncertain period following the Cold War. As President Obama put it in his Nobel lecture, "The plain fact is this: The United States of America has helped underwrite global security for more than six decades with the blood of our citizens and the strength of our arms." Now, however, the prospect of additional reductions in the size and capacity of U.S. military forces calls the "strength of our arms" into question: Will America continue to underwrite the great-power peace and the surge in human freedom and prosperity that it has secured?

The strategic success of the United States rests on achieving three things: the defense of the homeland, including all of North America and the Caribbean Basin; safe access to and the ability to exploit the "global commons," including the seas, the skies, space, and cyberspace; and a favorable balance of power across Eurasia. For all this to work as a "system," each piece must be in working order.

It took the attacks of September 11, 2001, to remind us not only that defense of the homeland comes first, but also that it requires the will and capacity to take the fight to the enemy. Osama bin Laden and his lieutenants may be getting long in the tooth, and their goal of driving the United States out of Muslim lands may be growing less probable by the day, but Sunni extremism will be with us for some time to come, as the Fort Hood shootings and the failed Times Square attack made evident. No matter how difficult a task, preventing al Qaeda and its allies from finding new nests in weak or sympathetic states is necessary if we are to protect America. Other tools of statecraft are important to this fight, but without sufficient military capability to take the fight to al Qaeda and its allies and project hard power in tough environs, these other tools will not carry the day.

The security of the commons—an awkward but nonetheless useful term—has long been regarded as an essential element in American strategy. But the protection of the realms outside the sovereign territory and waters of states is not just a strategic end in itself. It is the linchpin in America's capacity to keep the great-power peace and, in times of conflict, to dominate particular parts of the ocean, the sky, space, and the electromagnetic spectrum.

This is not a task that can be passed off to others or assured by treaties. To draw an analogy from city life, families and businesses need to know that police are present in order to feel confident that the streets are safe for routine activity; but they also need the police to be able to physically control the streets in emergencies or during spasms of illegal behavior. Compare life in most American cities with that in many northern Mexican towns, and the high cost of losing control of the urban commons becomes obvious. So, too, the international commons—be it the sea lanes to and from the Middle East or the atmosphere and cyberspace on which we depend for secure and instantaneous communication with our forces anywhere in the world. We would be foolish to take the peace of the commons for granted, along with the benefits we and others derive from it. Once we lose it, it will be extremely costly to regain.

The Balance of Geopolitical Power

The balance of geopolitical power among the states across the Eurasian landmass has always been a strategic interest of the United States. This was true even before the 20th century and the rise of America as a great power; [Founding Father] Benjamin Franklin's ability to play the French off against the British tipped the scales in the American Revolution. And in the last century, Americans paid an enormous price in blood and treasure to turn back German and Soviet bids for dominance in Europe and Imperial Japan's attempt to build an exclusive East Asian Co-Prosperity Sphere.

The current peace in Europe, fortunately, looks relatively durable. Russia's attempt to exert influence in the Caucasus and the "near abroad" is a security problem but one that should be manageable with a modicum of defense effort on our part and assistance to allies sitting on Russia's borders. That said, it does require some level of hard power both to deter [Russian prime minister Vladimir] Putin and his mafia from assuming they have free rein to intimidate surrounding countries and to reassure allies in Central and Eastern Europe that we have their backs.

But while Europe now is largely "whole and free" and far less of a security problem than it was in the 20th century, the "greater Middle East" has become a fundamental strategic concern of the United States. Initial attempts to address this concern by developing strategic partnerships with the shah of Iran or the ruling princes of Saudi Arabia produced no stable result. And so we have moved from an over-the-horizon posture to one of more direct involvement. The fact is, America's problems with Saddam Hussein's Iraq began well before 2003, and our interest in Mesopotamia will endure long after any "combat" troops leave. The prospect of an Iranian nuclear capability, frightening enough in itself, is perhaps more profoundly dangerous as a challenge to the stability of an inherently volatile region. Even if Iran is containable—even in the unlikely event that possession of nuclear weapons makes Tehran less prone than it is now to interfere in other nations—the response to an Iranian nuclear threat will most likely be to multiply the number of nukes across the region. Secretary of State Hillary Clinton's promise to extend American deterrence to the Gulf Arab states and others may be strategically sound if we fail to stop Iran's acquisition of a nuclear arsenal, but it is a commitment that will require even more involvement in the region—involvement backed by significant military power.

And now our strategic horizon has expanded to include South Asia. The war in Afghanistan has morphed into a broader concern about "AfPak," reflecting the fact that the problems of Pakistan are potentially of greater consequence than who rules in Kabul.

But the largest strategic conundrum of the post-Cold War era is the rise of China. Hundreds of millions of Chinese have been lifted out of poverty, and that is a human triumph and a success of the American-led international system. But while Beijing has an interest in sustaining this system, its zero-sum view of geopolitics and the pattern of its military modernization call into question its own longer-term goals, with consequences for America's leadership position in a part of the world that directly affects this country's future prosperity. No one desires to turn China into an enemy. But if history is any guide, failing to make clear to Beijing and the other Asian capitals that the United States has every intention of maintaining its military preeminence in the region will invite the kind of arms race and power politics among states that can only increase instability in the region, to the benefit of none.

Seen from this perspective, it should come as no surprise that the National Intelligence Council's *Global Trends 2025* report, reflecting the broad consensus across the U.S. intelligence community, concluded that the demand for American security guarantees would only rise in the future. What the Obama administration is creating is a gap between resources and strategy so significant that it will be impossible for the United States to meet those demands.

The National Security Strategy

The just-released Obama National Security Strategy reflects a drift toward a quite different approach, however. While it asserts that "there should be no doubt: the United States of America will continue to underwrite global security," it proceeds immediately to sigh, "We must recognize that no one nation—however powerful—can meet global challenges alone."

To be sure, the strategy states that there remains a need for U.S. leadership. But the tools it emphasizes—engagement, collective action, and partnerships—are emphasized as befitting a world in which mutual interests among states define the international scene. Given less attention is the traditional understanding that competition between democratic states and autocracies is the reality underlying our security requirements.

Similarly, the document notes the need to maintain America's "military superiority," yet it avoids linking that primacy to maintaining, or where possible expanding, "a balance of power that favors freedom"—a Bush administration phrase, but one fully consonant with America's grand strategy since the end of World War II. Frankly, ensuring America's role as the globe's leading military power is not an especially difficult goal to reach, given the declining defense budgets of most allies and the significant lead the United States has had over countries like Russia and China. However, being Number One in military capabilities is not the same thing as being preeminent globally and capable of deterring competitors, policing the international commons, and decisively defeating those who would go to war against us.

Although there are any number of sentences to be found in the National Security Strategy that point toward policy continuities with past administrations, the document's emphasis on the utility of soft power, on domestic renewal, and on issues unrelated to traditional national security concerns suggests a turning away from what have been the essential elements of America's longstanding approach to security matters. No one in the administration will admit as much, but the body language of how the administration is treating the likes of Iran, its lack of attention to our allies, and its unwillingness to even mention the word "China" as being of possible security concern all point toward a policy of strategic retrenchment. The administration's plans for defense spending give credence to this shift.

A Critical Juncture

But rather than have an honest debate over grand strategy, the administration is pursuing its vision by consigning the discussion of the defense budget to the narrow band of our country's financial health, as though our economic problems could be solved by reining in our supposed "imperial overstretch." But that is false. Defense spending is not the reason America's fiscal house is in disorder, and cutting defense could only be at best a marginal palliative.

Undermining America's ability to be the primary guarantor of global security, moreover, will create the conditions for greater competition among states and a more chaotic international environment. And it will inevitably lead the United States, for want of military capacity, to put off addressing security challenges until they became more difficult and costly to deal with.

Gates's speech at the Eisenhower Library was off the mark in many respects. The United States never became the "garrison state" many feared at the start of the Cold War, and even in the wake of the attacks of 9/11, the re-balancing of civil liberties and security has been minimal. Nor is the "military-industrial complex" a real problem. Defense companies now amount to less than 2 percent of Standard & Poor's total market capitalization for the country's 500 largest companies—hardly the dark and dangerous behemoth many on the left imagine.

But Gates was right in one respect: The nation is at a critical juncture when it comes to defense resources. The problem is the administration's response. If Obama and his team prevail, they will have created a spending dynamic that puts the United States on the same road as the countries of Europe, where domestic welfare crowds out all but minimal spending for defense. America's role in the world will decline, not because we have tried to do too much abroad, but because we have chosen to do too much at home. For less than a nickel on the dollar of U.S. GDP, we can maintain our preeminence in the world and, with prudent taxing and spending at home, revive America's economy as well. This shouldn't be an either/or choice. It hasn't been in the past, and America and the world have been the better for it.

Periodical and Internet Sources Bibliography

The following articles have been selected to supplement the diverse views presented in this chapter.

Joseph Antos	"Living in a Fiscal Fantasy World," *American Square*, July 12, 2011. www. americansquare.org.
Defending Defense Project	"Defending Defense: A Response to Recent Deficit Reduction Proposals," AEI, Heritage Foundation, and the Foreign Policy Initiative, November 23, 2011. www.aei.org.
Diana Furchtgott-Roth	"Obama's Green Jobs Lie," *Real Clear Markets*, November 3, 2011. www.realclearmarkets.com.
Jonah Goldberg	"How About Some Real Cuts?," *National Review* online, August 5, 2011. www.nationalreview.com.
John Goodman	"Are Entitlement Spending Cuts Bad for Young People?," National Center for Policy Analysis, January 18, 2012. www.ncpa.org.
Eli Lehrer and Ben Schreiber	"Go Green . . . By Cutting Government," *Weekly Standard*, September 12, 2011.
Gary Schmitt and Tom Donnelly	"Defining Defense Down," *Weekly Standard*, August 15–22, 2011.
Marc A. Thiessen	"A Secret Weapon to Save Defense," *Washington Post*, August 8, 2011.
Kevin D. Williamson	"Yes, Entitlement Spending Must Be Cut," *National Review Online*, April 5, 2011. www.nationalreview .com.
Fareed Zakaria	"Why Defense Spending Should Be Cut," *Washington Post*, August 3, 2011.

For Further Discussion

Chapter 1

1. Andrew G. Biggs and Jason Richwine argue that federal workers are overpaid, while John Gravois argues that too many federal jobs have been cut. Given the argument in each viewpoint, are their conclusions compatible? Why or why not?
2. Christopher J. Conover argues that the Patient Protection and Affordable Care Act will worsen inefficiencies in health care spending. What would Conover say in response to Jonathan Cohn's claim that the act is necessary to control Medicare spending?
3. Steven Hawkins admits that the relationship between spending on incarceration and education is correlative, not necessarily causal. Given this admission, what would Neal McCluskey say about Hawkins's call for increasing spending on education?

Chapter 2

1. Rich Lowry worries that a balanced budget amendment will not have adequate exceptions to allow for required military spending. How do you think Steven G. Calabresi would respond to Lowry's concern? Use textual passages from the viewpoints to support your answer.
2. Nicola Moore proposes that the growing debt-to-GDP (gross domestic product) ratio be halted by reform to entitlement spending. Do you think Henry J. Aaron would agree with her? Why or why not?

Chapter 3

1. Brian Riedl claims that government spending will not stimulate economic growth. What does Lawrence H. Summers

say in support of a payroll tax cut, which contradicts Riedl's claim?

2. What is the core disagreement regarding the debt between the view expressed by Michael Linden and Michael Ettlinger and the view of Andrew Foy and Brenton Stransky? What other information would you need to determine whose opinion you agree with?

Chapter 4

1. Andrew G. Biggs proposes raising Social Security's early retirement age to sixty-five, whereas David Rosnick says the normal retirement age should not be increased. Based on their viewpoints, are their opinions compatible or contradictory? Explain your answer.
2. Christian Parenti wants to use the government procurement process to invest in clean energy. How might Ronald Bailey object to this change in government procurement?
3. Thomas Eddlem contends that the United States should not be the world's policeman. Do Gary Schmitt and Tom Donnelly think it should be? Back up your answer with specific textual support.

Organizations to Contact

The editors have compiled the following list of organizations concerned with the issues debated in this book. The descriptions are derived from materials provided by the organizations. All have publications or information available for interested readers. The list was compiled on the date of publication of the present volume; names, addresses, phone and fax numbers, and e-mail and Internet addresses may change. Be aware that many organizations take several weeks or longer to respond to inquiries, so allow as much time as possible.

American Enterprise Institute for Public Policy Research (AEI)
1150 Seventeenth Street NW
Washington, DC 20036
(202) 862-5800 • fax (202) 862-7177
e-mail: info@aei.org
website: www.aei.org

The American Enterprise Institute for Public Policy Research is a private, nonpartisan, nonprofit institution dedicated to research and education on issues of government, politics, economics, and social welfare. AEI sponsors research and publishes materials defending the principles and improving the institutions of US freedom and democratic capitalism. AEI publishes *The American*, an online magazine, research papers, and its *AEI Outlook Series*, which includes *Economic Outlook*.

Brookings Institution
1775 Massachusetts Avenue NW
Washington, DC 20036
(202) 797-6000
e-mail: communications@brookings.edu
website: www.brookings.edu

The Brookings Institution is a nonprofit public policy organization that conducts independent research. The Brookings Institution uses its research to provide recommendations that advance the goals of strengthening US democracy, fostering social welfare and security, and securing a cooperative international system. The Brookings Institution publishes a variety of books, reports, and several journals, including the book, *Fiscal Therapy*. Commentary and a newsletter are available on its website.

Cato Institute
1000 Massachusetts Avenue NW
Washington, DC 20001
(202) 842-0200 • fax (202) 842-3490
website: www.cato.org

The Cato Institute is a public policy research foundation dedicated to limiting the role of government, protecting individual liberties, and promoting free markets. The Cato Institute's economic research explores the benefits of lower taxes, a significantly reduced federal budget, and less government involvement in market processes. Among the center's many publications available on its website is the study, "Will Obama Raise Middle-Class Taxes to Fund Health Care?"

Center for American Progress (CAP)
1333 H Street NW, 10th Floor
Washington, DC 20005
(202) 682-1611 • fax (202) 682-1867
website: www.americanprogress.org

The Center for American Progress is a nonprofit, nonpartisan organization dedicated to improving the lives of Americans through progressive ideas and action. CAP dialogues with leaders, thinkers, and citizens to explore the vital issues facing the United States and the world. CAP publishes numerous research papers, which are available at its website, including, "Budgeting for Growth and Prosperity."

Center on Budget and Policy Priorities (CBPP)
820 First Street NE, Suite 510
Washington, DC 20002
(202) 408-1080 • fax (202) 408-1056
e-mail: center@cbpp.org
website: www.cbpp.org

The Center on Budget and Policy Priorities is a policy organization working at the federal and state levels on fiscal policy and public programs that affect low- and moderate-income families and individuals. The center conducts research and analysis about proposed budget and tax policies to ensure that the needs of low-income families and individuals are considered in public debates. There are many reports and policy briefs available on its website, including "Emergency Unemployment Insurance Benefits Remain Critical for the Economy."

Center for Freedom and Prosperity (CF&P) and Center for Freedom and Prosperity Foundation
PO Box 10882
Alexandria, VA 22310-9998
(202) 285-0244
e-mail: info@freedomandprosperity.org
website: www. freedomandprosperity.org

The Center for Freedom and Prosperity is a nonprofit organization created to lobby lawmakers in favor of market liberalization. The Center for Freedom and Prosperity Foundation is a nonprofit educational organization that publishes studies and conducts seminars analyzing the benefits of jurisdictional tax competition, financial privacy, and fiscal sovereignty. The Center for Freedom and Prosperity Foundation publishes the *Prosperitas* study series, which includes, "Government-Run Health Care Means Higher Deficits and Debt."

Citizens for Tax Justice (CTJ)
1616 P Street NW, Suite 200
Washington, DC 20036
(202) 299-1066 • fax (202) 299-1065
e-mail: ctj@ctj.org
website: www.ctj.org

Citizens for Tax Justice is a public interest research and advocacy organization focusing on the impact of federal, state, and local tax policies. CTJ fights for fair taxes for middle and low-income families, requiring the wealthy to pay their fair share, and closing corporate tax loopholes. CTJ publishes numerous reports, including, "Policy Options to Raise Revenue."

Competitive Enterprise Institute (CEI)
1899 L Street NW, Floor 12
Washington, DC 20036
(202) 331-1010 • fax (202) 331-0640
e-mail: info@cei.org
website: www.cei.org

The Competitive Enterprise Institute is a nonprofit public policy organization dedicated to advancing the principles of limited government, free enterprise, and individual liberty. CEI aims to craft and deploy media advocacy campaigns around that foundation of solid research to reach policy makers, influential opinion leaders, and grassroots activists. CEI publishes a policy brief series, short policy white papers, and issue analyses, all available at its website.

Economic Policy Institute (EPI)
1333 H Street NW, Suite 300, East Tower
Washington, DC 20005-4707
(202) 775-8810 • fax (202) 775-0819
e-mail: epi@epi.org
website: www.epi.org

The Economic Policy Institute is a nonprofit Washington, DC, think tank that seeks to broaden the discussion about economic policy to include the interests of low- and middle-income workers. EPI briefs policy makers at all levels of government; provides technical support to national, state, and local activists and community organizations; testifies before national, state, and local legislatures; and provides information and background to the media. EPI publishes books, studies, issue briefs, popular education materials, and other publications, among which is the biennially published *State of Working America*.

Heritage Foundation
214 Massachusetts Avenue NE
Washington, DC 20002-4999
(202) 546-4400 • fax (202) 546-8328
e-mail: info@heritage.org
website: www.heritage.org

The Heritage Foundation is a conservative public policy organization dedicated to promoting policies that align with the principles of free enterprise, limited government, individual freedom, traditional US values, and a strong national defense. The Heritage Foundation conducts research on policy issues for members of Congress, key congressional staff members, policy makers in the executive branch, the news media, and the academic and policy communities. The Heritage Foundation has hundreds of reports, factsheets, testimonies, and commentaries available on its website.

Institute for Research on the Economics of Taxation (IRET)
1710 Rhode Island Avenue NW, 11th Floor
Washington, DC 20036
(202) 463-1400 • fax (202) 463-6199
e-mail: callen@iret.org
website: www.iret.org

The Institute for Research on the Economics of Taxation is a public policy research organization dedicated to the belief that constructive, free-market economic policies are essential for the nation's economic progress. IRET conducts research and analysis of the economic effects of tax, budget, and regulatory public policy initiatives and offers guidance to policy makers. IRET publishes frequent congressional advisories, including, "Health Bills' Tax Increases Would Harm Health Care And The Economy."

National Taxpayers Union (NTU)
108 North Alfred Street
Alexandria, VA 22314
(703) 683-5700 • fax (703) 683-5722
e-mail: ntu@ntu.org
website: www.ntu.org

The National Taxpayers Union is a nonprofit, nonpartisan citizen organization working for lower taxes and smaller government. NTU aims to mobilize elected officials and the general public on behalf of tax relief and reform, less wasteful spending, individual liberty, and free enterprise. NTU publishes news and action alerts on its website, including, "Modest Spending Restraint Can Balance the Budget in Ten Years."

Tax Foundation
National Press Building
529 14th Street NW, Suite 420
Washington, DC 20045-1000
(202) 464-6200
e-mail: tf@taxfoundation.org
website: www.taxfoundation.org

The Tax Foundation is a nonpartisan educational organization working to educate taxpayers about sound tax policy and the size of the tax burden borne by Americans at all levels of government. The Tax Foundation aims to gather data and publish information on the public sector in an objective, unbiased fashion. Its publications include *Fiscal Facts*, background papers, and special reports such as, "How Is the Patient Protection and Affordable Care Act Paid For?"

United for a Fair Economy (UFE)
29 Winter Street
Boston, MA 02108
(617) 423-2148 • fax (617) 423-0191
e-mail: info@faireconomy.org
website: www.faireconomy.org

United for a Fair Economy is an organization that works to narrow the wealth gap in the United States. UFE provides media capacity, face-to-face economic literacy education, and training resources to organizations and individuals that work to address the widening income and asset gaps in the United States. Overviews of issues and links to resources are available on its website, including, *Fair Play, Responsible Wealth Action News*, and *Tax Fairness Action News*.

Urban Institute
2100 M Street NW
Washington, DC 20037
(202) 833-7200
website: www.urban.org

The Urban Institute works to foster sound public policy and effective government by gathering data, conducting research, evaluating programs, offering technical assistance overseas, and educating Americans on social and economic issues. The Urban-Brookings Tax Policy Center, a joint venture of the Urban Institute and Brookings Institution, provides analysis and facts about tax policy to policy makers, journalists, citizens, and researchers. The Urban Institute publishes policy briefs, commentary, and research reports, all available on its website.

Bibliography of Books

Bruce R. Bartlett	*The New American Economy: The Failure of Reaganomics and a New Way Forward*. New York: Palgrave Macmillan, 2009.
Leslie Carbone	*Slaying Leviathan: The Moral Case for Tax Reform*. Washington, DC: Potomac Books, 2009.
Menzie D. Chinn and Jeffry A. Frieden	*Lost Decades: The Making of America's Debt Crisis and the Long Recovery*. New York: W.W. Norton, 2011.
Tom A. Coburn	*The Debt Bomb: A Bold Plan to Stop Washington from Bankrupting America*. Nashville, TN: Thomas Nelson, 2012.
Jim DeMint	*Now or Never: Saving America from Economic Collapse*. New York: Center Street, 2012.
Patrick Fisher	*The Politics of Taxing and Spending*. Boulder, CO: Lynne Rienner, 2009.
Elizabeth Garrett, Elizabeth Grady, and Howell E. Jackson	*Fiscal Challenges: An Interdisciplinary Approach to Budget Policy*. New York: Cambridge University Press, 2008.
Garet Garrett	*Insatiable Government*. Caldwell, ID: Caxton Press, 2008.

John Steele Gordon — *Hamilton's Blessing: The Extraordinary Life and Times of Our National Debt: Revised Edition*. New York: Walker & Co., 2010.

Michael J. Graetz — *100 Million Unnecessary Returns: A Simple, Fair, and Competitive Tax Plan for the United States*. New Haven, CT: Yale University Press, 2010.

Mike Lee — *The Freedom Agenda: Why a Balanced Budget Amendment is Necessary to Restore Constitutional Government*. Washington, DC: Regnery Publishers, 2011.

Paolo Mauro — *Chipping Away at Public Debt: Sources of Failure and Keys to Success in Fiscal Adjustment*. Hoboken, NJ: Wiley, 2011.

Michael Moran — *The Reckoning: Debt, Democracy, and the Future of American Power*. New York: Palgrave Macmillan, 2012.

Grover Glenn Norquist — *Leave Us Alone: Getting the Government's Hands Off Our Money, Our Guns, Our Lives*. New York: W. Morrow, 2008.

Benjamin I. Page and Lawrence R. Jacobs — *Class War? What Americans Really Think About Economic Inequality*. Chicago: University of Chicago Press, 2009.

Scott W. Rasmussen — *The People's Money: How Voters Will Balance the Budget and Eliminate the Federal Debt.* New York: Threshold Editions, 2012.

Leah Rogne, Carroll Estes, Brian R. Grossman, and Brooke Hollister — *Social Insurance and Social Justice: Social Security, Medicare, and the Campaign Against Entitlements*. New York: Springer, 2009.

Irene S. Rubin — *The Politics of Public Budgeting: Getting and Spending, Borrowing, and Balancing*. Washington, DC: CQ Press, 2010.

Robert Scheer — *The Pornography of Power: Why Defense Spending Must Be Cut.* New York: Twelve, 2009.

Rob Simpson — *What We Could Have Done with the Money: 50 Ways to Spend the Trillion Dollars We've Spent on Iraq*. New York: Hyperion, 2008.

Matthew Sinclair — *How to Cut Public Spending.* London: Biteback, 2010.

Peter J. Tanous and Jeff Cox — *Debt, Deficits, and the Demise of the American Economy*. Hoboken, NJ: Wiley, 2011.

John B. Taylor — *First Principles: Five Keys to Restoring America's Prosperity.* New York: W. W. Norton, 2012.

Richard E. Wagner — *Deficits, Debt, and Democracy.* Northampton, MA: Edward Elgar, 2012.

Thomas E. Woods Jr.	*Rollback: Repealing Big Government Before the Coming Fiscal Collapse*. Washington, DC: Regnery, 2011.
Robert E. Wright	*One Nation Under Debt: Hamilton, Jefferson, and the History of What We Owe*. New York: McGraw-Hill, 2008.

Index

O

P